Classic
Fairy Tales

Classic
Fairy Tales

Capella

This edition published in 2006 by Arcturus Publishing Limited
26/27 Bickels Yard, 151–153 Bermondsey Street,
London SE1 3HA

ISBN-13: 978-1-84193-287-3
ISBN-10: 1-84193-287-6

Editor: Rebecca Gerlings
Designer: Jane Hawkins
Translator: Translate-A-Book

Printed in China

Classic
Fairy Tales

Contents

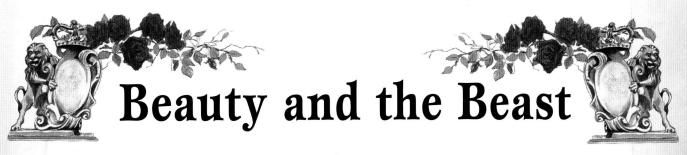

Beauty and the Beast

ONCE UPON A TIME, IN A RICH COUNTRY,
a powerful merchant had three very beautiful daughters.
The two older sisters became prouder and more selfish every
day, but the youngest was so kind and sweet that everyone called
her "Beauty". Every week, several young men came to the rich
merchant's house to ask for the hand of one of his three daughters.
But the two elder sisters replied that they would only marry a duke
or a count. As for Beauty, she told them that she was too young
and that she wanted to keep her father company for a while longer.

Alas, one day the merchant lost all his fine
possessions. He summoned his
daughters and told them:

"My poor children, all we have
left is an old shack in the country.
We shall have to go and live there."

The two elder sisters flew into a rage and stamped their feet in vain; their father was completely ruined and they had to accept it. Soon, the whole family left for the country to live in the wretched shack. Beauty did everything she could to help her father. Hard work and fresh air made her become even more beautiful. But her two sisters were bored and spent their time grumbling.

One day, the merchant told his daughters that he had to go to town for a while on business. The two elder sisters jumped for joy:

"Oh! Father, please bring us back some dresses and hats. We've got nothing left to wear!" they cried.

The merchant promised, then he turned to Beauty and asked her: "And how about you, Beauty?"

"I'd like you to bring me a rose, because roses do not grow here," the girl replied softly.

Then the merchant embraced his daughters and left for the town.

8

A few days later, when he had
settled his affairs, he set off home
again. He had to pass through a
great dark forest, and the night took him by surprise, causing him to become
lost. It was snowing and the wind was so strong that the merchant thought
he was going to die of cold. Suddenly, he saw a light shining in the distance.
He gathered the last of his strength and set off through the storm in the
direction of the light. Soon, he arrived at a magnificent castle. As the
heavy door was open, he went in. Inside there was an eerie silence.

"Hello? Is anyone there?" called the merchant.

But no one replied. Intrigued, he pushed open a door on his right and entered a splendid room hung with tapestries and thickly carpeted. There was a fire in the great fireplace, and a table was laid before it. Countless dishes laden with delicious food were set out before a single place-setting. The merchant was starving so he could not resist.

"The lord of this castle will forgive my boldness," he said to himself as he sat down at the table. Soon midnight struck and still no one had appeared ... Rather anxiously, the merchant started to explore the deserted castle. He came to a bedroom, lay down on the great bed and fell into a deep sleep. Next morning, when he woke up, he found, to his amazement that new clothes had been laid out for him on a chair, and an ample breakfast awaited him on a table.

"Thank you, sir," said the merchant out loud to his invisible host, and sat down to eat.

Then, when he had breakfasted well, the merchant prepared to go on his way.

10

As he passed a bush bearing bright red roses, he remembered his younger daughter and cut off the most beautiful branch for her. Suddenly, there was a sound like a thunder-clap. The merchant turned round and found himself facing a creature so horrible that he nearly fainted. Although he was dressed in an elegant doublet, the monster had an enormous lion's head with huge sharp teeth. His great hairy paws had massive claws and his panting breath was harsh and fierce.

"Ungrateful man!" roared the Beast. "I saved your life and welcomed you into my castle. And now you steal what is most precious to me in all the world: my roses. Because of this outrage, you will die, sir."

"My Lord, forgive me," begged the merchant. "I did not mean to offend you. I wanted to take these flowers to one of my daughters, who asked me for some."

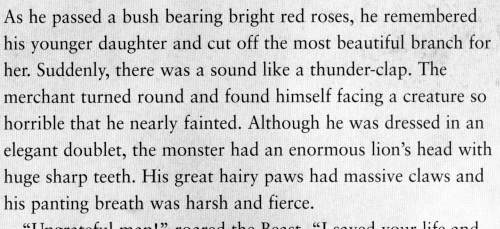

"Don't call me 'my Lord'. My name is the Beast!" roared the monster. "But … you have daughters, you say? You can keep your life, on condition that one of them comes here of her own free will to die instead of you. If they refuse, you will come back yourself. Otherwise my vengeance will be terrible."

11

The poor man did not want to
sacrifice one of his daughters, but this
respite at least enabled him to return and
embrace them one last time. So the merchant
accepted and, with a heavy heart, he went
home. When he arrived his daughters ran to
embrace him. But as he offered the branch of roses
to Beauty, he burst into tears and said:

"Beauty, take these roses, they have cost your poor
father dearly!"

And he told them of his terrible adventure. No
sooner had he finished his story than the two elder
sisters turned on Beauty:

12

"Why didn't you ask for dresses, like we did?" they screamed. "Look what misfortune you have brought upon us: because of you, our father is going to die and you are not even sorry!"

"Weeping would be useless," replied Beauty. "Our father will not die. Since the Beast is willing for one of us to take our father's place, I will give myself up to him."

The merchant pleaded and protested but the girl would not yield. And so with sad farewells, she left her family and set out on her way. When she arrived at the castle, night had already fallen and the huge building was plunged into a deep silence.

Beauty pushed open the door and went in. Immediately, there was a sound like a thunder-clap and the Beast appeared. Beauty thought she would die of terror. But the monster spoke to her in a voice that he tried to make sound gentle:

"Your sacrifice is admirable and I admire your courage. Follow me, I beg you. I will take you to your room."

When he had done so, the Beast bowed respectfully to Beauty and took his leave.

"The Beast must have dined already tonight. But tomorrow he
will probably kill me and eat me," thought the girl before she fell asleep.

Next morning, as no one came to fetch her, Beauty decided to take a look
around the castle. Although she was terrified at the idea of meeting the Beast at
any moment, she could not help marvelling at the splendour of the palace.

To her surprise, on one of the doors she read a sign that said: "Beauty's
Drawing Room". She went in and found herself in the most beautiful room she
had ever seen. A huge library filled a whole wall. Broad armchairs were set
round a piano and a delicious breakfast was laid out on a delightful round
table. But above all, a delicate scent pervaded the whole room, because there
were enormous bunches of red roses everywhere. Beauty spent a very pleasant
day reading and playing music.

When evening
came she went to the great hall of
the castle and found the table laid for two. As
she was taking her seat, the Beast appeared with his
customary clap of thunder.

"Beauty, would you allow me to dine with you?" he asked her.

"You are the master," replied Beauty.

"No," replied the Beast, "you are the mistress here. Tell me, you find me very ugly, don't you?"

Beauty, who never told lies, replied awkwardly:

"That's true. But I believe that you are good."

The monster did not reply. Then he took a mirror out of his pocket and handed it to Beauty, saying:

"This is for you. It's a magic mirror. Any time you want, you can see your family in it."

Beauty took the mirror and saw her father standing in front of his hovel. His eyes were filled with sadness. Beauty's heart was wrung, but she thanked the Beast and went on with her supper, feeling less fearful than before. Then suddenly, he asked her another question:

"Beauty, would you agree to be my wife?"

Although she was scared of rousing his anger, Beauty replied trembling: "No, Beast."

"So farewell, Beauty," said the Beast sorrowfully, as he left the room.

"Alas," Beauty wondered sadly, "why is he so ugly, when he seems so good? I couldn't possibly marry him. So it seems I must die!"

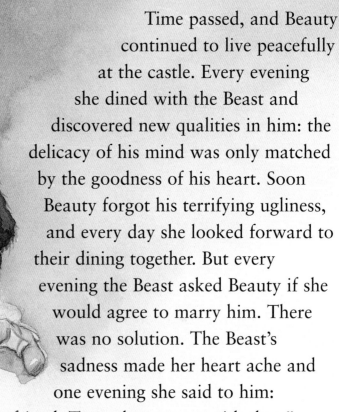

Time passed, and Beauty continued to live peacefully at the castle. Every evening she dined with the Beast and discovered new qualities in him: the delicacy of his mind was only matched by the goodness of his heart. Soon Beauty forgot his terrifying ugliness, and every day she looked forward to their dining together. But every evening the Beast asked Beauty if she would agree to marry him. There was no solution. The Beast's sadness made her heart ache and one evening she said to him:

"Beast, I will always be your friend. Try to be content with that."

"I'll have to be," replied the Beast, "but promise never to leave me."

Beauty was upset at his words. In her mirror she had seen that her father was now very ill.

"Beast, I long to see my father again. I shall be so unhappy if you won't allow me that joy," she begged.

"I don't want you to suffer," replied the Beast. "So go back to your father, even if I have to die of grief because I can't see you any more. You can leave tomorrow. Take this ring. When you want to come back here, just lay it on a table. So, farewell, Beauty."

Beauty promised to come back a week later, then she went up to bed. When she woke up next morning, she found she was already at her father's house. The poor merchant wept for joy to see his daughter. But her two sisters nearly choked with jealousy when they saw their sister so happy and even more beautiful than when she had left them. Together they decided to prevent Beauty returning to the Beast.

"The monster will fly into a rage when he finds she has not kept her promise and he will take revenge on her," they said to one another.

At the end of the week, when it was time for Beauty to leave, her two sisters tore out their hair, pretending to be in despair, so Beauty gave in to them. She agreed to stay for another week. But on her tenth night at her father's house, Beauty saw the Beast in a dream. He was lying in the castle garden and he was dying. Then she realized she could not stay away from him any longer. She got up, lay the ring on the table and went back to bed.

When she woke up next morning she was back at the Beast's castle. She waited impatiently for evening to come, but the Beast did not appear at dinner. Wild with anxiety, Beauty remembered her dream and ran into the garden. She found the Beast lying on the grass. Forgetting his hideous ugliness, she threw herself upon him, sobbing. Gently the Beast opened his eyes and said in a dying voice:

"Beauty, why didn't you keep your promise?
I am dying of the grief you have caused me. But I
die happy because I can see you once more."

"No, Beast, you shan't die!" cried Beauty.
"You are going to live and become my husband!
I thought I only felt friendship for you and now I
see that I can't live another day without you."

Scarcely had Beauty uttered these words, when a flash of lightning struck the Beast. Beauty screamed in terror and hid her face. But when she opened her eyes again, instead of the Beast, she saw a young prince standing before her, who was handsome as the day.

"Beauty," he said tenderly, "a witch condemned me to go about in the shape of a monster until a beautiful woman agreed to marry me. You alone were touched by my good heart and were able to overlook my ugliness."

Their wedding was celebrated the very next day. Thanks to the prince, Beauty's father's wealth was restored to him. As for her two sisters, they threw themselves at Beauty's feet and begged her forgiveness. And being very generous, she granted it.

Beauty lived for many years with the prince. They had many children and they were all very happy because their hearts were full of goodness.

THE END

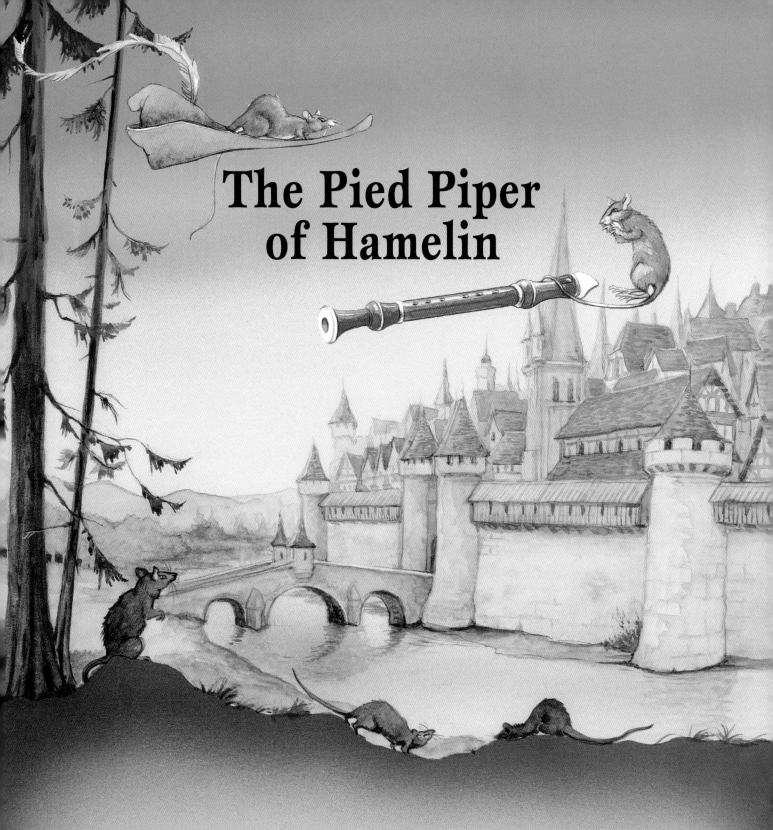

The Pied Piper
of Hamelin

ONCE UPON A TIME, A LONG TIME AGO, THERE WAS a small town in Germany called Hamelin. It was a prosperous town of rich merchants and wealthy traders. The people wanted for nothing: their granaries were full of corn and their cellars had the biggest barrels of wine in the region. Life in Hamelin was good.

Then, one day, a terrible calamity struck the town. A big, black rat appeared. It had a pointed muzzle and red eyes. At first, the inhabitants did not pay it much attention. But then a second rat arrived, then a third, then a fourth! Within a few days, the town was over-run by thousands of rats. The streets, squares, even the houses were swarming with the nasty creatures. These rats were not afraid of anything.

They fought the dogs, bit the horses, attacked the cats, and when people tried to chase them away with a broom or a shovel, they came back moments later in even greater numbers.

The situation was becoming intolerable. The inhabitants were becoming more and more worried, so they decided to call a meeting in the town hall square, to try and find a solution.

"This can't go on," one of them said. "The rats are eating up everything. Soon we won't have anything left in our winter stores!"

"Before the rats came, Hamelin was a clean, quiet town. Look at the state these creatures have got us into," added another.

"We must drive out the rats as quickly as possible. This has gone on too long," they all shouted together.

The crowd was becoming more and more restless. In order to calm them down, the mayor of Hamelin came out of the town hall and addressed them:

"Dear fellow citizens, we are going through a difficult time. But I am sure that in the end these rats will leave the town."

"Well, just what are you going to do to get rid of them?" demanded the unhappy people.

"I'm going to call together my councillors to come to a decision," he replied.

But the inhabitants of Hamelin had already waited too long and demanded an immediate solution. Saying the first thing that came into his head, the mayor took out a big purse from his pocket and said:

"Here is a purseful of gold. I am prepared to give it to the person who will get rid of the rats for us."

A great silence fell on the town hall square. People were busy thinking about what they could do with a purseful of gold. But none of the inhabitants of Hamelin actually knew how to get rid of the rats. Just then, a voice was raised from the middle of the crowd.

"I – the Pied Piper – am prepared to take on the job." Everybody looked with astonishment at the one who had just spoken. It was the first time he had been seen in the town. Tall and slender, the man had strange piercing eyes and a long, very thin moustache. He wore strange clothes, too, in bright colours, and held a flute between his fingers.

"Can you get rid of all the rats in the town for us?" asked the mayor, amazed.

"Certainly. And I guarantee that they won't come back," said the stranger.

The townsfolk of Hamelin were dumbfounded. The mayor himself did not know what to think.

"Well, since you know what to do, get to work! What are you waiting for?" he said.

"First we must settle one last detail. That purseful of gold seems but poor payment to me. I demand a gold piece for each rat that leaves the town," said the Pied Piper.

A murmur ran through the crowd.

"A gold piece for each rat!" cried the mayor. "But that's impossible! There must be several hundred or even several thousand rats in Hamelin!"

"There are a million of them," said the Pied Piper calmly. "And I will not work for less than a million gold pieces."

"I need to think this over. I will call together my councillors … It is an enormous sum that you are asking for!"

"I give you till tomorrow morning," replied the Piper with a smile.

The mayor summoned his councillors urgently.

"This man is our last hope. But paying him a gold piece for each rat seems an awful lot to me," he told them.

"We shall have to put up the taxes. The people will become discontented and choose another mayor," said one of the councillors anxiously.

"But wait a minute, who's talking about paying him?" cried the mayor. "We can easily accept his proposal, let him do his work, and then drive him out of the town afterwards without paying him anything."

28

All the councillors applauded and the mayor went back to the town hall square, very satisfied with his mean plan. He found the Piper sitting by the fountain, polishing his flute.

"Stranger," said the mayor, "we are agreed. We will pay the price you ask if you succeed in getting rid of the rats for us. When can you begin?"

"This very night," said the Piper. "Order everyone to stay indoors." The mayor went home, very proud of his scheme. The inhabitants of Hamelin were lucky to have such a clever mayor! His wife and six sons were waiting for him at home, in tears. They had spent all day trying to drive the rats out of their house, but in vain.

"Don't worry any longer. Tomorrow this nightmare will be over, there won't be a single rat left in the town," promised the mayor.

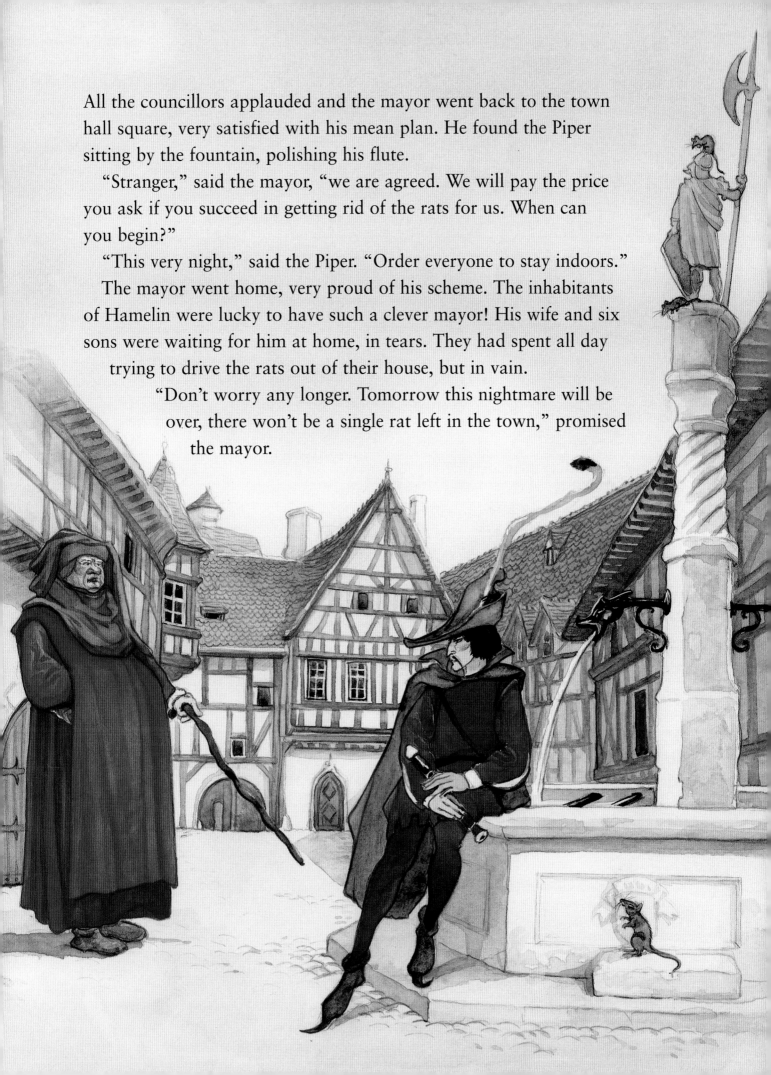

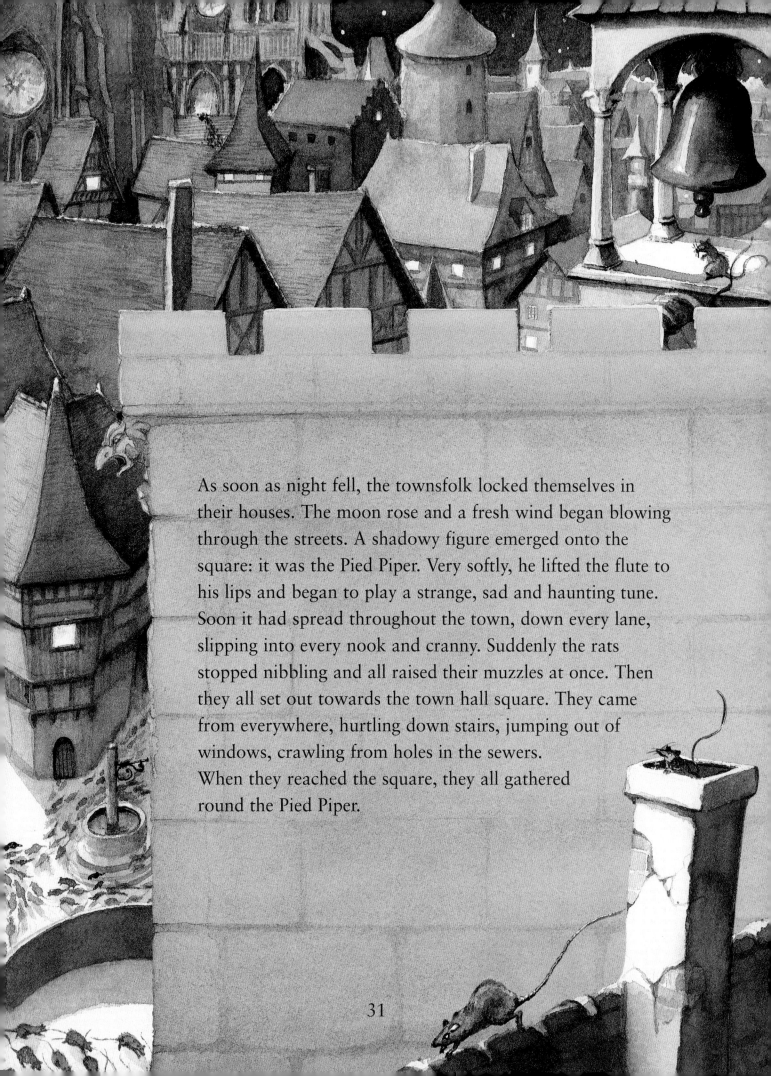

As soon as night fell, the townsfolk locked themselves in
their houses. The moon rose and a fresh wind began blowing
through the streets. A shadowy figure emerged onto the
square: it was the Pied Piper. Very softly, he lifted the flute to
his lips and began to play a strange, sad and haunting tune.
Soon it had spread throughout the town, down every lane,
slipping into every nook and cranny. Suddenly the rats
stopped nibbling and all raised their muzzles at once. Then
they all set out towards the town hall square. They came
from everywhere, hurtling down stairs, jumping out of
windows, crawling from holes in the sewers.
When they reached the square, they all gathered
round the Pied Piper.

Very slowly,
the Piper
began walking
towards the town gates,
playing his flute all the while. Noiselessly,
the throng of rats followed him, as if hypnotized.
    From their windows, the inhabitants of Hamelin watched the
creatures flood past, and they too were struck dumb with amazement.

The Piper walked to the river Weser, which ran outside the town. He stopped at the water's edge and looked at the mass of rats spread out before him, every one of them staring at him with beady eyes. Suddenly he commanded them:

"Jump!"

And without hesitating for a moment all the rats flung themselves into the freezing water and disappeared one after another. When not a single rat was left on the bank, the Pied Piper stopped and went back into the town. The night was dark and all the inhabitants were asleep.

Next morning, at daybreak, the Pied Piper knocked on the mayor's door. After a long pause, the mayor answered the knock. He was still in his dressing gown and was wearing a nightcap.

"There is not a single rat left in the town," announced the Piper. "I have come to claim what is due to me: a million gold pieces."

"And where have the rats gone? How can I tell that they have gone for good?" asked the mayor.

"I drowned them in the Weser. I kept my part of the bargain. Now you must pay me," the stranger insisted.

"What? I must pay for disappearing rats! I told you I would pay a gold piece for each rat, but I meant real dead ones. You were supposed to bring them here to me!"

With that, the mayor slammed the door. The Pied Piper stared with his piercing eyes at the door that had been shut in his face. Inside he heard a small child talking in his sleep and an idea took shape in his mind.

34

"I will surely find a way of making them pay for my services," he muttered. And he turned on his heel and walked away.

A little later, the mayor, in very good humour, went to the town hall and summoned all the inhabitants of Hamelin to the square. When everyone had arrived, he spoke:

"Dear fellow citizens, I have rid Hamelin of the scourge that had fallen upon it: today there is not a single rat left in the town! To celebrate this success, I invite you all to a great banquet tonight at the town hall." That evening, the people of Hamelin got ready to attend the mayor's banquet. They put their children to bed and went off to the town hall. There they drank, ate and danced all through the night. Meanwhile, the Pied Piper wandered alone through the town streets.

The moon rose and a
fresh little wind began
blowing. The Piper lifted
his flute to his lips and
began to play a merry,
lively tune that spread
even to the darkest and most
forgotten alleyways. Suddenly the
house doors opened…

36

...and the children poured out to gather round
the Pied Piper. Then he began walking towards the town gates,
playing all the while. The children followed, smiling and humming.
They did not take their eyes off him, just as if they had been
hypnotized. Soon, the Piper came to the river Weser. He
crossed the bridge with all the children and began
climbing the mountain on the other side. Still the
children followed him and did not seem to
feel at all tired. The bigger ones carried
the smaller ones and they were all
laughing and dancing together.
Soon, every one of them had
disappeared into the night.

Early next morning, when the inhabitants of Hamelin returned home from the town hall, they searched in vain for their children. The mayor of Hamelin ran through all the rooms of his house, desperately calling for his six sons, but they had gone. Then he found a piece of paper nailed to his door, on which was written:

"Received on account for the disappearance of one million rats: 253 children from the town of Hamelin."

It was signed: "The Pied Piper."

The mayor became wild with distress. The children of Hamelin were never seen again, but even today, on misty evenings, when the moon rises and a fresh little wind begins blowing, far off in the mountain, you can hear a strange tune played on a flute and the echo of children's laughter. From that day on, the mayor of Hamelin always kept all his promises, down to the last detail.

THE END

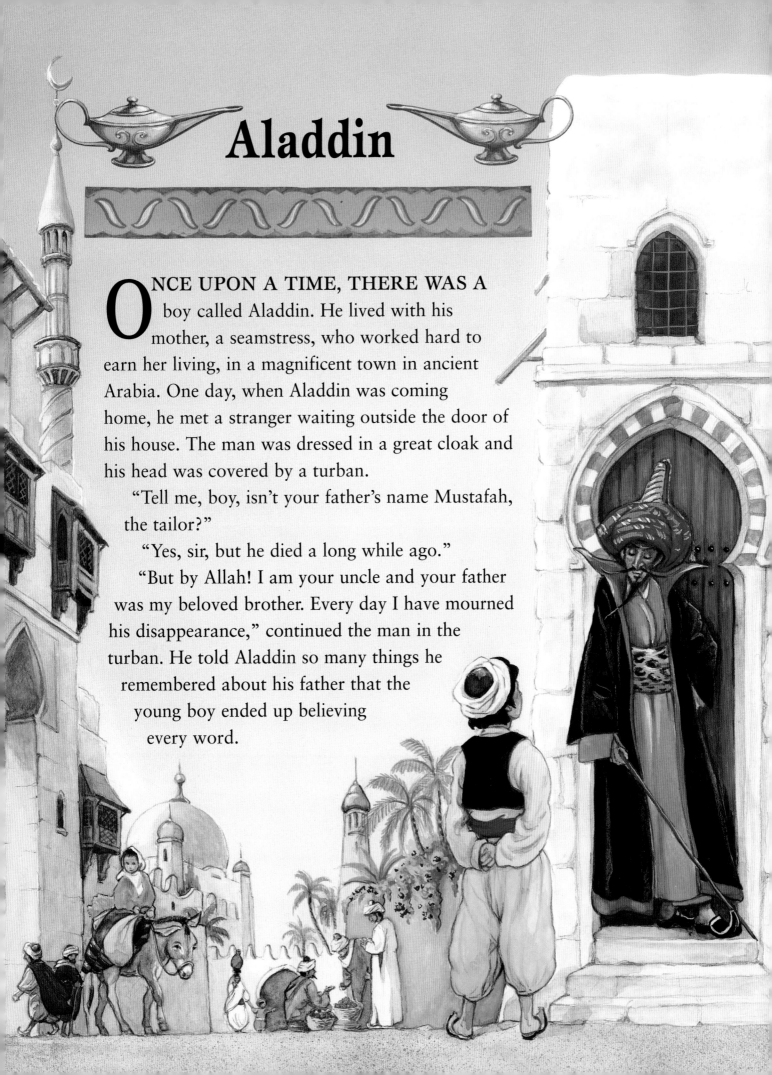

Aladdin

ONCE UPON A TIME, THERE WAS A boy called Aladdin. He lived with his mother, a seamstress, who worked hard to earn her living, in a magnificent town in ancient Arabia. One day, when Aladdin was coming home, he met a stranger waiting outside the door of his house. The man was dressed in a great cloak and his head was covered by a turban.

"Tell me, boy, isn't your father's name Mustafah, the tailor?"

"Yes, sir, but he died a long while ago."

"But by Allah! I am your uncle and your father was my beloved brother. Every day I have mourned his disappearance," continued the man in the turban. He told Aladdin so many things he remembered about his father that the young boy ended up believing every word.

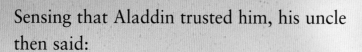

Sensing that Aladdin trusted him, his uncle
then said:

"Follow me to the mountain and I will
reveal my secrets to you."

Aladdin could not resist his curiosity and followed him into the
mountains. His uncle, who was an African magician, lit a great fire,
onto which he threw some magic perfume, as he recited some magic
words. Suddenly, the sun trembled and with a terrifying rumble the
earth opened. Aladdin bent down and saw a big slab of stone with a
metal ring set in it. Seeing Aladdin looked frightened, the magician
said to him:

"Don't be afraid, nephew. Under this stone lies a hidden treasure
that will make you the richest man in the world. Pull the ring!"

40

As soon as Aladdin had pulled the ring, the slab lifted to reveal a staircase.

"Go down it!" ordered the magician. "When you come to a magnificent garden, you will find another staircase. Climb it and you will find a lamp set in a recess, which you must bring back to me."

As Aladdin still hesitated to go down the stairs, the magician gave him a ring and added:

"Take this ring, it will protect you from ill fortune."

Aladdin put the ring on his finger and ventured down the staircase into the cave.

Soon he found himself in an extraordinary garden, where the branches of the trees were covered in rubies, opals, emeralds and diamonds. Then he found the second staircase and, at the top, he came upon a wonderful lamp shining in its recess. Aladdin picked it up, hid it under his shirt and returned the way he had come.

The magician was waiting for him at the top.

Aladdin held out his arms to be
helped out of the cave.

"Help me, please."

"Give me the lamp!" replied the
magician harshly.

"First help me out!" said Aladdin.

"You will not get out unless you give me
the lamp!" hissed the magician.

As Aladdin refused, the magician
turned red with fury and cast a magic
spell so that the heavy slab closed
and Aladdin found himself
imprisoned in the cave.

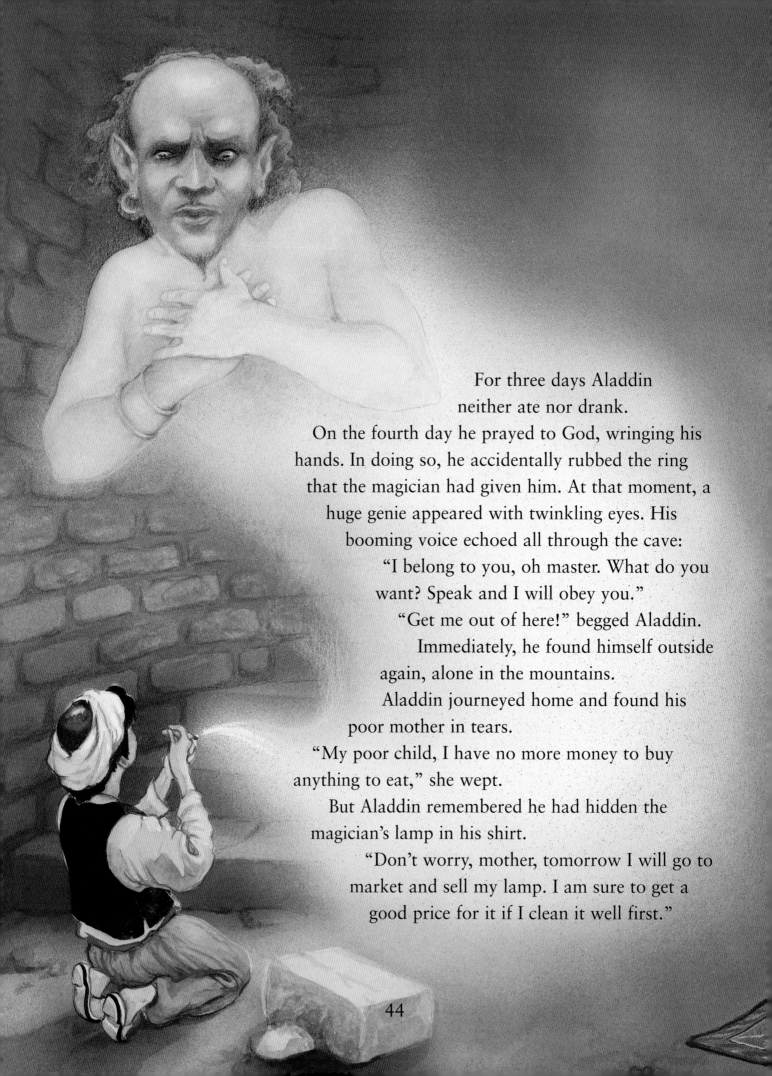

For three days Aladdin
neither ate nor drank.
On the fourth day he prayed to God, wringing his
hands. In doing so, he accidentally rubbed the ring
that the magician had given him. At that moment, a
huge genie appeared with twinkling eyes. His
booming voice echoed all through the cave:
"I belong to you, oh master. What do you
want? Speak and I will obey you."
"Get me out of here!" begged Aladdin.
Immediately, he found himself outside
again, alone in the mountains.
Aladdin journeyed home and found his
poor mother in tears.
"My poor child, I have no more money to buy
anything to eat," she wept.
But Aladdin remembered he had hidden the
magician's lamp in his shirt.
"Don't worry, mother, tomorrow I will go to
market and sell my lamp. I am sure to get a
good price for it if I clean it well first."

Aladdin took out
his lamp and began
polishing it when, without
warning … a huge genie appeared, even
more alarming than the first. His eyes were red as
glowing embers and his beard was black as coal.
Aladdin plucked up courage and spoke
firmly to him:
"We're hungry, bring us something
to eat."

The genie presented him with a
delicious meal served on a
silver plate and immediately
disappeared in a puff of smoke.
Aladdin's mother gazed in
wonder at the lamp, then she
sat down to eat with her
son. From that day
onwards they never
knew hunger again.

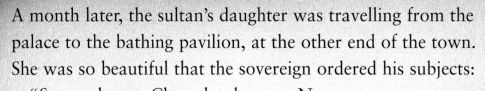

A month later, the sultan's daughter was travelling from the palace to the bathing pavilion, at the other end of the town. She was so beautiful that the sovereign ordered his subjects:

"Stay at home. Close the shutters. No one must see my daughter."

But Aladdin had decided otherwise. He got into the bathing pavilion and hid behind a column. When the princess arrived, she approached the bath and raised her veil. Then Aladdin could see her in all her beauty. Her eyes were enormous and full of kindness, and her shapely face was framed by her long brown hair.

Immediately, Aladdin fell deeply in love with the princess, and swore to ask the sultan for her hand the very next day. As soon as the sun had risen, Aladdin went to the palace, where he was granted an audience. When he entered the throne room, he bowed respectfully to the sultan:

"Your Majesty, may I have the hand of your daughter?"

The sultan burst out laughing:

"What impudence you have to come before me and make such a request! If you are so keen to marry my daughter, prove it by sending an army to be my personal bodyguard!"

And so he dismissed Aladdin.

47

When Aladdin got home, he remembered the wonderful lamp and the genie. He rubbed the lamp and the genie soon appeared.

"Genie, I want you to bring me an army of eighty soldiers on horseback and eighty slaves bearing sacks of silver and gold."

At once the genie produced everything he had been asked to provide.

"Follow me to the palace!" the delighted Aladdin ordered all the soldiers and slaves.

When they arrived at the palace courtyard, they were met by an enthusiastic crowd. The slaves threw fistfuls of silver and gold coins at the onlookers who were cheering Aladdin on his way. Alerted by all the noise, the sultan appeared on the palace steps and could not believe his eyes. He was so impressed by such splendour that he immediately granted his daughter's hand to Aladdin.

The next day, Aladdin married the princess and the sultan gave the biggest party the kingdom had ever seen. The bride and groom set up home in a sumptuous palace and lived there happily for many years.

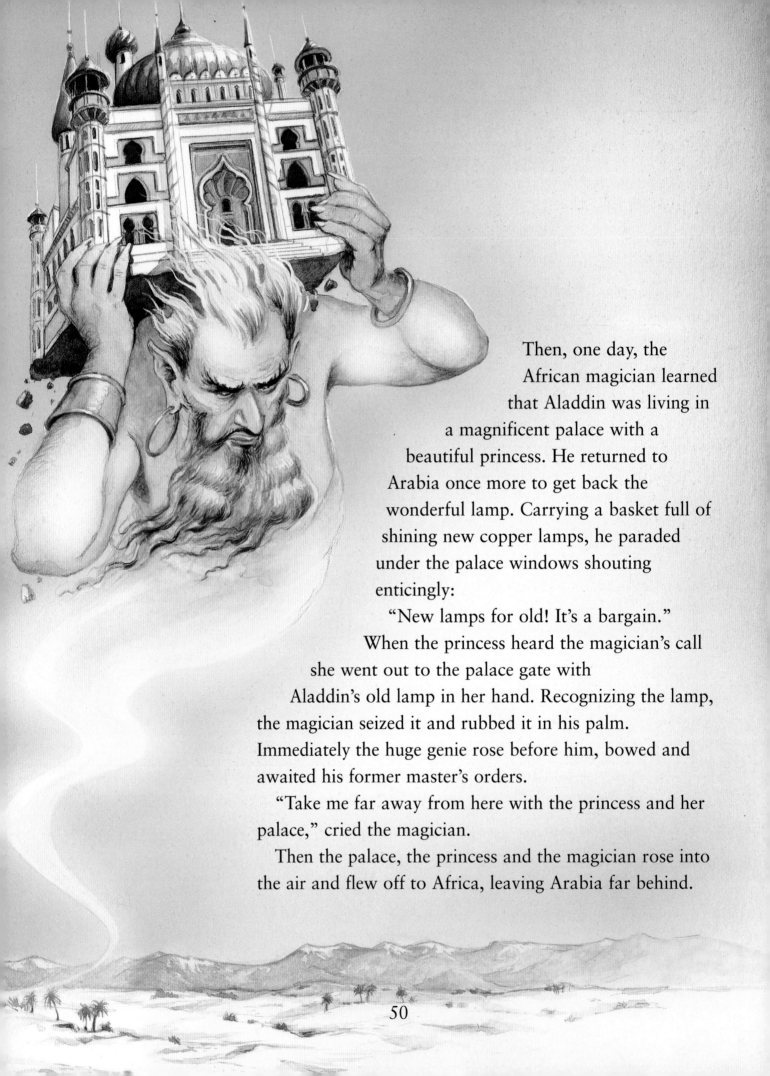

Then, one day, the
African magician learned
that Aladdin was living in
a magnificent palace with a
beautiful princess. He returned to
Arabia once more to get back the
wonderful lamp. Carrying a basket full of
shining new copper lamps, he paraded
under the palace windows shouting
enticingly:

"New lamps for old! It's a bargain."

When the princess heard the magician's call
she went out to the palace gate with
Aladdin's old lamp in her hand. Recognizing the lamp,
the magician seized it and rubbed it in his palm.
Immediately the huge genie rose before him, bowed and
awaited his former master's orders.

"Take me far away from here with the princess and her
palace," cried the magician.

Then the palace, the princess and the magician rose into
the air and flew off to Africa, leaving Arabia far behind.

When the sultan awoke, he sent for his daughter
only to discover she had disappeared. Furious, he summoned Aladdin.

"What have you done with my daughter, you accursed villain?"

In vain, Aladdin tried to explain to the sovereign that he knew nothing
about the kidnapping of the princess. The grief-stricken sultan would not
listen to him.

"Bring her back to me immediately or I will have your head cut off!"

"Your Majesty, give me forty days and I will bring back your daughter,"
begged Aladdin.

"Agreed," replied the sultan. "But if you have not brought back my
daughter in forty days, you will die a horrible death."

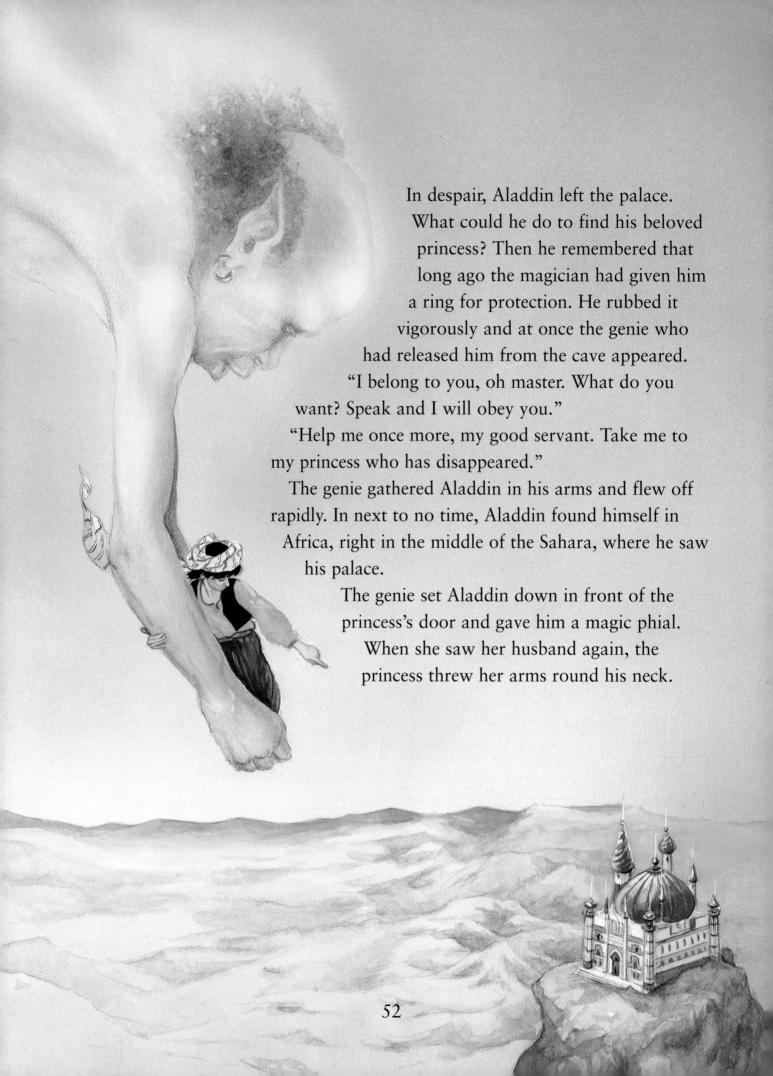

In despair, Aladdin left the palace.
What could he do to find his beloved
princess? Then he remembered that
long ago the magician had given him
a ring for protection. He rubbed it
vigorously and at once the genie who
had released him from the cave appeared.
"I belong to you, oh master. What do you
want? Speak and I will obey you."

"Help me once more, my good servant. Take me to
my princess who has disappeared."

The genie gathered Aladdin in his arms and flew off
rapidly. In next to no time, Aladdin found himself in
Africa, right in the middle of the Sahara, where he saw
his palace.

The genie set Aladdin down in front of the
princess's door and gave him a magic phial.
When she saw her husband again, the
princess threw her arms round his neck.

"Aladdin, forgive me. It is all my fault. I exchanged your old lamp for a new one…"

She began to weep, but Aladdin reassured her:

"Do not worry, my dear wife. We will get back the wonderful lamp and return home. This is what you are going to do: choose your finest clothes and prepare a feast for the magician. Serve the very best wine. Then pour the contents of this phial into his glass so that he will fall asleep forever."

The princess followed Aladdin's instructions to the letter and invited the magician to a wonderful meal. Charmed by the princess's invitation, the magician ate plentifully and drank back his glass of wine in one go.

Straightaway, he dropped into a deep sleep. Aladdin came out of the cupboard where he had been hiding and took back the wonderful lamp.

He stroked it with his hand and the genie appeared.

"Take us home, powerful genie. To the sultan's country, and quickly!" he ordered.

The palace rose into the air and flew off towards Arabia.
Aladdin and his princess gazed in wonder as countries and
oceans passed beneath them. The genie set down the palace
in its former place. Wild with joy, the sultan ran to his
daughter and embraced her tenderly. Then he begged Aladdin's
pardon and ordered a month of rejoicing to celebrate the
couple's return.

They both lived happily in their palace and had many
children, who were the most beautiful ever seen in the country.
As for Aladdin, he swore always to take great care of his
wonderful lamp and magic ring.

THE END

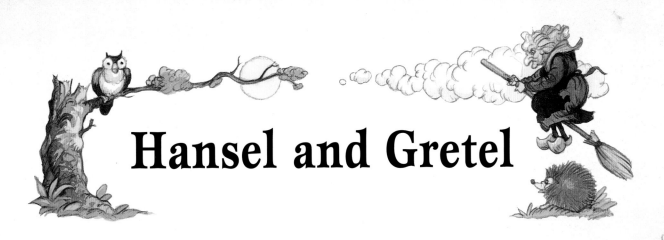

Hansel and Gretel

ONCE UPON A TIME, LONG AGO, THERE WAS AN
unfortunate woodcutter, who lived with his family in a little house,
built of wood and thatch, at the edge of a great enchanted forest.
His first wife was dead and he had remarried a woman who was always
in a bad temper. Nevertheless, he was happy because his first wife had given
him two lovely children: a good and brave son called Hansel and a beautiful
daughter called Gretel.

One year, the country was hit by a terrible famine. When winter came, the unfortunate woodcutter's larder was empty.

"What is going to become of us? We have no more bread to feed our children. We must find a solution quickly, otherwise we will die of hunger," said the woodcutter, sadly.
Then, his cruel wife had a terrible idea:
"Tomorrow, at sunrise, we will take Hansel and Gretel very deep into the enchanted forest and leave them there. They will never be able to find their way home and we shall be well rid of them! Thus we shall have two mouths less to feed…"

"But I couldn't do such a thing! They are my children," cried the woodcutter.

"So you'd rather die of hunger!" his wife retorted harshly.

The poor woodcutter shed a thousand tears but, terrified of this wicked woman's temper, he finally gave in. In the next room, Hansel and Gretel, who were supposed to be asleep, heard their stepmother's cruel words. Little Gretel began to sob:

"Oh, my poor brother, I don't want to be left in that terrible forest. I am so frightened of witches!" Hansel took his little sister in his arms, hugged her tight and comforted her.

"Don't be afraid, little sister. Grandfather taught me how to track our way home. We'll get out of it!"

During the night, Hansel got out of bed. Making sure that his father and stepmother were fast asleep, he crept into the garden, gathered some small white pebbles, then went back to bed without making a sound. Early next morning, their stepmother opened the children's bedroom door and called them sharply:

"Come on, up you get, you lazybones! We are going to gather wood in the forest!"

Gretel put on
her old apron and tried to blink back her tears. In his
pocket Hansel held on tight to the little pebbles he had gathered.
The cruel stepmother was in such a hurry to lose the two children that she
ran along the road to the enchanted forest! Hansel followed her, throwing
down his precious white pebbles behind him as he went. After a very long
walk, the wicked stepmother stopped.

"Lie down beneath that oak tree and when I have finished working I
will come back and fetch you," she said in a soft, dishonest voice.

Hansel knew that their horrible
stepmother was lying, and that she would never
come back. He lay down under the great oak tree with
his little sister. Shivering with cold, they fell asleep.
When Hansel and Gretel woke up again, it was night
and sure enough, no one had come to fetch
them. An icy wind was blowing and
Gretel began to cry because she was
so frightened.

"Be brave, Gretel," said Hansel.

"When the moon shines we will be able to see the pebbles that I threw down on the path. We will find our way back and be home by morning." The two children walked all night through the forest, following the trail of little white pebbles, praying that they would not meet any witches. They arrived home at dawn. The woodcutter was wild with joy to get his children back. He hugged them tight and kissed them. Hansel and Gretel were so happy to be back with their father that they forgot all about being tired and hungry.

But when she saw them, their stepmother gave them a vicious scolding:

"Where have you been, you brats? You disobeyed me! Your father and I have been sick with worry!"

Hansel and Gretel did not answer their stepmother, which only increased her rage. Exhausted, they went to their bedroom and lay down on their beds to rest. The woodcutter's wicked wife waited for a few moments, pushed the bedroom door to make sure the children were asleep and then she turned to her husband:

"Tomorrow morning we will take them even further into the enchanted forest and this time Hansel and Gretel will be lost forever. They will never find their way home and we shall be well rid of them!"

62

The unhappy woodcutter tried to protest, but his wife started shouting:

"Look around you! We have nothing to eat. All that's left is one tiny crust of bread. I am not going to die of hunger because of your greedy children. There is no other solution."

The woodcutter shed a thousand tears, but finally gave in to his wife once more. Fortunately, Hansel had overheard their conversation. He tried to go out into the garden to look for pebbles again, but this time, the house door was locked. So he went back to bed and sought another idea. Next day, before the sun rose, the stepmother went to wake the children. She gave each of them a tiny piece of bread and then led them even deeper than before into the enchanted forest.

As Hansel had no pebbles this time, he had to throw crumbs from his piece of bread onto the path. When night fell, Hansel and Gretel were alone once more, abandoned in the heart of the forest. The moon began to shine and the two children looked everywhere for the breadcrumbs which were meant to show them the way home. Alas, the birds had eaten all the crumbs! There was no trace of them! The children wandered for three long days and three long nights, completely lost in the huge forest. Exhausted and starving, Gretel fell to the ground.

"We are lost and we are going to be eaten by witches," she said, beginning to cry.

Despite his courage, Hansel was also very frightened. Horrible things were said about the witches of the forest, which froze his blood with terror. Not knowing what to do, he and Gretel lay down to rest. Next morning, the tuneful song of a robin redbreast awoke the children. Hansel took his little sister by the hand and they set out again in the hope of finding their way home. They hadn't gone far before they saw smoke coming out of a chimney. There was a house nearby and someone was at home.

"We are saved! We are saved!" cried the children.

As they approached the house,
they saw to their delight that it was made entirely of
sweets and cake. The roof was tiled in chocolate.
The chimney was made of nougat. And the walls were built of
gingerbread, coated with jam.

Hansel loved nougat, so he climbed onto the roof
and ate up part of the chimney. Gretel greedily
licked the walls covered with jam.
They had never eaten such
delicious things! But suddenly
they heard a strange voice from
inside the house:

"Nibble-mouse, nibble-mouse, who is nibbling at my house?"

"It's the wind! It's the wind!" the children replied, laughing.

"It sounds more like children to me. And how I love children. So come in and sit down at my table and I'll serve you a feast fit for a king!"

Hansel and Gretel were still hungry, so they rushed straight into the kitchen. The house door banged shut and a horrible witch stood before them. Her back was hunched, her teeth were black, her hair was like spiders' webs and there was a large wart on her ugly nose. The witch caught Hansel by the arm and threw him into a cage. Then she tied Gretel to the table leg.

"Hee! Hee! Hee!" she cackled. "Now it's my turn for a feast. I'm going to eat you but, so that I enjoy you even better, I'll wait until I have fattened you up."

For the first few days, Hansel and Gretel managed not to eat the sweets and pastries that the witch gave them. But after a while, Hansel was so hungry that he threw himself upon all the delicious treats that she had to offer.

After a week, Hansel had become quite plump and the horrible witch decided he was now fat enough to become her dinner.

"Oh! Scrumptious! This boy promises to be … succulent!" she hissed, looking greedily at her prisoner.

She lit the fire to cook poor Hansel. He was trembling with fear. Then she untied Gretel, who seemed just as scared as Hansel.

"Climb into that oven, my girl," she said, "and tell me if it is hot enough yet to cook your brother in. Hee! Hee! Hee!"

"But I have never climbed into an oven before and I don't know how to. Can you lift me up?" asked Gretel, innocently.

"Stupid girl! Look, the oven doorway is so big that I could get in myself."

So saying, the cruel witch climbed into the oven. Gretel quickly slammed the oven door tight. The witch began to burn, and screamed horribly. The little girl grabbed the cage key from its hook, and rushed to set Hansel free.

"I've thrown the witch into the oven, she is dead, we are free!" she cried, hugging her brother.

In the witch's living room stood a shining chest. Curious, Hansel and Gretel opened it. Inside they found magnificent jewels and sacks filled with countless gold pieces. Never was there so much wealth in a single chest!

The children filled their pockets with the treasure and ran off. Outside in the forest, the sun was shining. Hansel and Gretel, who were stronger now, finally found their way home. When they arrived, their father could not hold back his tears, he was so happy. He had been feeling very lonely without his children, and their wicked stepmother was dead!

Gretel untied her apron and thousands of diamonds fell out. Hansel turned out his pockets and a shower of gold pieces tumbled onto the floor. Thus, with all the witch's money, they never knew hunger or poverty again, and for many years afterwards, Hansel and Gretel lived happily with their father on the edge of the enchanted forest.

THE END

Peter Pan

ONCE UPON A TIME IN LONDON, THERE LIVED A
little girl whose name was Wendy. She lived with her parents and her
two brothers, John and Michael. Wendy had a very vivid imagination,
and every evening before they went to sleep, she would tell them a story.

One evening the children's parents went out. Wendy, John and Michael
were already asleep, so they didn't notice when the window opened and the
bedroom curtains parted gently to admit a strange young boy into the room.
He looked about him keenly and seemed to be searching for something.

"There it is, Tinker Bell! I've seen it. She slid it under the chest of drawers!" cried the boy, addressing his words to a strange little golden light that hovered nearby.

If you looked closely, you could see that this light was in fact a beautiful little fairy. When she flapped her wings, she let fly a light cloud of gold dust. In their hasty search, the boy and the fairy knocked over a chair.

Wendy awoke with a start, just as the fairy, Tinker Bell, slipped into a drawer to hide.

"But who are you?" Wendy asked the silhouette that she could just make out in the dark.

"My name is Peter Pan," replied the boy, still looking under the chest of drawers.

"What are you looking for under there?"

"My shadow. It's run away again! I spend my time running after it. I've already tried sticking it to my heels, but it always manages to break away!"

"Well then, we'll have to sew it on!" said Wendy, jumping out of bed.

She ran and fetched a needle and thread from the drawing room.

"How did you get in here?" she asked her new friend, as she began sewing his shadow onto his foot.

"Well, I just flew to the window and opened it," Peter Pan replied, simply.

As Wendy did not seem to believe a word Peter Pan was telling her, he explained some more:

"I live in Never Never Land with the Lost Boys. They are children who fell out of their prams when they were tiny. Come with me to Never Never Land," Peter Pan begged her. "The Lost Boys need a mother so badly!"

"But I can't leave my brothers all alone!"

"Well, they can come with us," replied Peter Pan, happily.

Peter Pan taught Wendy, John and Michael to fly. And, when everyone was ready, they took off into the clouds with Tinker Bell the fairy. How they enjoyed racing the birds and sliding down the rainbows!

Second on the right and then straight on till morning: that was the way Peter Pan and his new friends went, until Never Never Land appeared on the horizon. No sooner had they landed than a crowd of children threw themselves upon them, laughing! They were all dressed in bear skins that made them so fluffy and roly-poly that it was impossible to catch them. Wendy thought she would be squashed flat and even Peter Pan found it very difficult to call them to order.

"Listen everybody, I've brought you a mother! We are going to take her to our cave and you are going to behave very well for her."

To enter the Lost Boys' cave, the children had to crawl inside a hollow tree trunk. Then they let themselves slide down at top speed until they dropped into the middle of their underground home. Wendy, John and Michael soon got used to their new life. Wendy was kept busy looking after the children, doing the washing and mending their clothes. She made sure they were in bed by seven o'clock every evening and told them all a story before they fell asleep.

One day, when Wendy
and Peter Pan had taken the boys
to the mermaids' lagoon, the sky
suddenly grew dark and they saw a great ship
appear, whose captain, draped in a voluminous black
cape, looked most sinister. He was giving orders to his
ship's boy, who was tying up a beautiful dark-haired girl.

"Tie her up tight and attach stones to her ankles. She
must not be able to float. She must drown!"

"It's Captain Hook," explained Peter Pan to Wendy, who was clinging on as tightly as possible to him.

"Look! He has a hook instead of his right hand. That's because I cut off his hand in a duel and threw it to the crocodile!"

Wendy was terrified.

"He has captured Tiger Lily, the Indian Chief's daughter! We must save her!" cried Peter Pan, thrilled at the thought of confronting his enemy, Captain Hook, once more.

In the twinkling of an eye, he had flown to the boat and was taunting the pirate Captain:

"So, Captain, have we made this trip for our health!"

Mad with rage, Captain Hook turned round. The ship's boy took fright, jumped into the water and disappeared. Peter Pan took Captain Hook to a rock that was as slippery as soap. The fight was unequal: the boy kept fluttering here and there, attacking him from all sides, while Captain Hook made the air around him whistle as he slashed about with his terrible iron hook, without ever hitting his adversary. Suddenly, the Captain slipped and fell into the water. Then a tick-tock sound could be heard coming nearer and nearer. Captain Hook had another mortal enemy apart from Peter Pan: it was the crocodile who had swallowed his hand after the duel … and had swallowed his watch with it! Captain Hook let out a yell and swam off as fast as he could.

Peter Pan ran to free Tiger Lily, the Indian Chief's daughter. Then, together with Wendy and the children, they took her back to her father's camp, where the Indians lived. Peter's band were welcomed as heroes. Sitting in a circle round the fire, they smoked the peace pipe.

It was very late when Peter Pan, Wendy and the children returned to their underground house. Wendy put the children to bed and hugged them one by one. Then Michael asked her:

"Tell me, Wendy, are you really our mother now?"

Wendy realized that soon Michael would have forgotten his real father and mother and that they ought to go back to London as soon as possible.

"Peter, we have to go home," she said.

"Just as you like, Wendy," Peter replied curtly. Tinker Bell will show you the way."

"You're not coming with us, Peter?" asked Wendy.

"Go to London with you? Of course not! I am not going to risk growing up at any price!"

Wendy understood that only those who lived in Never Never Land remained children forever. But she had made her decision.

It was very sad to say goodbye. Peter pretended not to care, but Wendy knew that inside he was feeling very unhappy.

They were about to leave the cave, when they heard
a terrible roaring outside. Furious at his defeat, Captain Hook had
launched a final attack on the Indian camp. The children could not
get out until the battle was over. If the Indians won, they would
beat their tom-toms to signal that the way was clear.

The Indian braves fought like lions but, taken by surprise, they
were defeated by the treacherous pirates. Captain Hook had won,
but this victory was not enough for him, he was really after Peter
Pan and his band. But how could he flush them out of their
underground house?

Then Captain Hook played a mean trick: he ordered the tom-toms to be beaten. Inside the cave, there was a great whoop of joy:

"The tom-toms! Indian victory!" shouted Peter Pan and the children.

Believing their way was clear, John went out first. One of the pirates tied him up in a sack and threw him into the ship's hold. Next, they caught Michael and Wendy. Tinker Bell was captured using a butterfly net. None of the four prisoners had time to call out and warn Peter Pan. Quaking with terror, the three children were now tied to the ship's great mast. As for Tinker Bell, she had been locked in a bird-cage. Gloating with triumph, Captain Hook was already thrilled at the thought of throwing them to the crocodiles. But he decided to put off the execution till the next morning and he went to bed instead.

While the Captain slept, Tinker Bell
managed to escape from her cage and flew as quickly
as she could to warn Peter Pan. The boy did not
hesitate for a moment, but rushed to help his friends.
When he arrived aboard the pirate ship, all was quiet and
the only sound that could be heard was the tick-tock of the
crocodile circling the ship; confident that a fine feast was being
made ready for him.

As soon as they saw him arrive, the children recognized Peter
Pan. But he signalled them to be quiet and set them free in
silence: he wanted to surprise Captain Hook in his sleep. He
crept softly towards the Captain's cabin, opened the door and
yelled out loud:

"This time, Captain, it's you or me!"

Captain Hook jumped out of bed, but Peter Pan hit him hard in the right spot and he doubled over. Woken by the noise, the pirates had started to struggle with John and Michael. But the two boys had had time to steal their weapons from them and their victory was easy. So Captain Hook and Peter Pan were left alone, face to face, for a final duel.

"Young upstart," cried Captain Hook, "your last hour has come!"

"No, you villain," replied the boy, "you had better look out for yourself!"

85

Their swords clashed during a long exchange. Little by little, Peter Pan pushed the Captain to the edge of the ship, finally forcing him up onto the railings.

"Push him over, Peter! Push him over!" shouted the children.

Peter Pan gave a little kick and toppled Captain Hook overboard where he fell straight into the crocodile's waiting jaws.

Then Peter Pan ordered the ship to set sail for London. Exhausted by the battle, Wendy, John and Michael fell asleep on the bridge and remembered nothing of their return journey. When the sun rose on London the next day, they were far from Never Never Land, safely back in their little beds and, when they woke up, it was already time to get up for school.

THE END

Robin Hood

ONCE UPON A TIME, THERE WAS AN ENGLISH
king called Richard who was so good and brave that he had
been nicknamed Richard the Lionheart. His castle stood on a
huge estate at the edge of Sherwood Forest. The forest was dense
with great trees and thick undergrowth. It was a very dangerous
place for anyone who wandered into it by chance.

King Richard spent his days happily in the company of his
daughter, the beautiful Lady Marion. But Richard's jealous brother,
Prince John, sought only one thing: to take over the throne. The day
came when enemies declared war on England and good King
Richard had to go off to battle.

Cruel and greedy, Prince John immediately seized power and sent his own soldiers all over the kingdom. They looted and pillaged wherever they went, and plunged the people of England into desperate poverty. Prince John also forbade hunting in Sherwood Forest. Those who broke this law were immediately hanged.

One morning, a friend of Prince John, Lord Guy of Gisborne, met some guards who had just arrested a poacher.

"Have mercy, my Lord," pleaded the unfortunate wretch. "We live in terrible poverty. I killed this rabbit only to feed my family."

"You have broken the law, so you shall be hanged," replied Lord Guy.

But no sooner had he uttered these words than a sharp arrow whizzed through the air and struck the earth between his horse's feet.

"Who dares to defy me thus?" roared Guy of Gisborne.

"I do, Lord Guy of Gisborne!" cried a voice from the treetops.

Then a vigorous young man, with a friendly, smiling face jumped down from the tree where he had been hiding. His dark green clothes matched the colour of the leaves. His eyes gleamed with mischief and his hands firmly held a bow whose arrow was pointed at Guy of Gisborne.

"Who are you? And how do you know my name?" barked Lord Guy.

"My name is Robin Hood and I know the names of all those who are traitors to our good King Richard. Release your prisoner, sir, and your guard's life will be safe."

"Never! Take hold of him!" Guy of Gisborne ordered his men furiously.

But before the guards could move a step nearer, a shower of arrows rained down on them. A companion of Robin Hood was hiding behind each tree. The guards ran off, abandoning Guy of Gisborne, who had fallen from his horse in the attack. Then Robin grabbed a heavy purse full of gold pieces that was buckled to Lord Guy's belt. He gave it to the prisoner and turned to Guy of Gisborne:

"My Lord, remember that Robin Hood robs rich men like you to give to the poor."

With these words Robin vanished into the forest.

That same evening, Prince John was dining in the company of his friends, and Guy of Gisborne told them about his misadventure. All the guests agreed that Robin Hood was a dangerous rebel and that he had to be stopped. Only one person, a beautiful young woman, remained silent with downcast eyes. Her lovely face looked sad. It was Lady Marion, King Richard's daughter. Since her father had gone away to war, she had been a powerless witness to the cruel actions of her uncle, Prince John.

The weeks went by. Every day Robin Hood
robbed some rich man to bring happiness to the
poorest. Prince John became exasperated. He gathered his knights
together to set a trap for Robin Hood.

"In a few days the spring festival will take place. Let's arrange an
archery contest. Robin Hood is a brilliant archer. He will not be able
to resist the challenge. We will take advantage of the occasion to seize
him," declared Lord Gisborne.

"And we'll arrest him in a public place!" exclaimed Prince John.
"At last the people will understand that it is I who rule England!"

All the knights approved of this idea. Only Lady Marion sat in
nervous silence.

In Robin's camp, deep in Sherwood Forest, his friends advised him
not to take part in the competition.

"Guy of Gisborne will recognize you and have you
arrested!" said Little John, a great-hearted giant of a man.

92

"I can't resist the chance to teach them a lesson," Robin replied smiling.

"We all know that you are the best archer in all England, Robin, but I think showing yourself in the open like that is very dangerous," replied Friar Tuck, a monk who was as wise as he was stout.

"I will go in disguise so that I am not recognized," declared Robin, and he added mischievously, "if you are afraid I'll go alone."

"Alone! Certainly not!" his companions exclaimed in a single voice.

The day of the festival came. In a clearing in the forest, a
platform had been set up for the archery contest. Prince
John took his seat. Lady Marion stood at the back.
Disguised as a beggar with a big hat pulled over his eyes,
Robin Hood came up to the platform. His eyes met those of
the Lady Marion. Immediately he fell in love with her and
his mind was made up. Robin Hood would win the
tournament for the love of the beautiful Marion. For her
part, Lady Marion had noticed this strange young man. His
ragged clothes made him look poor, but nothing in his
shining eyes spoke of sadness or hunger.

The tournament began. Throughout
the whole day one archer followed
another until only two were left in the
contest. The first of these, called Hubert and reputed to be
invincible, stood up bravely, flexed his bow and aimed. The crowd held
its breath. Hubert released the arrow and it planted itself exactly in the
middle of the target. Prince John stood up and said:

"I think that would be difficult to beat."

Without showing the least concern, the remaining competitor took
his place. He flexed his bow and, hardly bothering to take aim, he shot.
His arrow whizzed like lightning, split Hubert's arrow in two and
planted itself in the exact centre of the target. The crowd roared.
Prince John himself applauded and held out the trophy.

"Come forward, stranger, the prize is yours."

"Will you allow me to present it to someone close to my heart?"
asked the ragged stranger.

Then going up to Marion,
he knelt down respectfully and said to her:

"Please accept this modest gift as a token of my love."

"But who are you, sir?" she asked.

Then the man stood up, took off his hat and proudly announced:

"Robin Hood, at your command, Lady Marion, and at King
Richard's service!"

"Arrest him!" shouted Prince John, mad with rage.

But, quick as a flash, Robin Hood plunged into the crowd, which
parted to allow their hero to escape, then closed up again forming an
impenetrable barrier.

Back in their forest camp, Robin said to his band of men:

"We must be on our guard, friends. After an incident like that, Prince John will certainly be after us."

His companions took it in turns to keep watch. Robin himself perched on the highest branch of a great oak. Night fell. Suddenly, there was a rustling in the bushes. A young monk came out of the shadows, his face concealed by his hood. Robin jumped down from the oak tree and barred his way.

"Halt, holy man, what are you doing here?" he asked.

When the monk did not reply Robin grew angry:

"Tell me what you are doing here or I'll make you!"

"Well, let's see about that," said the monk, drawing a sword.

And there, in the darkness, the fight commenced. Robin quickly saw that he was facing an adversary almost as skilful as himself, and a lot lighter.

"Let's stop this stupid fight," he declared after a few moments. "You defend yourself well. Come and join Robin Hood, for you are worthy to become one of his company."

"Are you really Robin Hood?" asked the monk, standing motionless.

"Certainly," replied Robin, laughing.

Then the monk slowly lifted the hood covering his face and said:

"Don't you recognize me, Robin?"

It was Lady Marion.

Stunned, Robin knelt down at her feet. That is how Marion joined Robin Hood's company in Sherwood Forest. When Prince John heard the news, he flew into a terrible rage. He was determined to put an end to the rebels of Sherwood and summoned his whole army:

"Invade Sherwood Forest!" he ordered. "Flush these traitors from their den and take them as far as possible from their camp. I want them all dead. For my part, I will go with my guard to deal with Lady Marion in person. When I have taken her prisoner, Robin Hood will be sure to surrender, and both of them shall be hanged."

That same day, a terrible battle raged in Sherwood Forest. Summoning every ounce of their courage, Robin Hood's companions fought like lions. But Prince John's soldiers were more numerous and better armed, so they had the upper hand. Meanwhile, Prince John had reached the camp where Lady Marion awaited the outcome of the battle.

"I am delighted to meet you again, niece," he said, laughing cruelly, "This time you won't get away from me so easily."

"Don't come near me, you fiend," screamed Marion, as Prince John grabbed her arm.

Without warning, an arrow whistled past Prince John's ear.

"Coward! Aren't you ashamed of yourself for attacking a woman?" asked Robin, emerging from a thicket. "Come and stand up to me instead!"

But already Prince John's guards had fallen upon Robin. Alone against ten, he was quickly overcome by force. Prince John's soldiers were still busy tying Marion's hands when suddenly a knight appeared, accompanied by his bodyguards, all dressed in black.

"What is going on?" asked the black knight. "Who are these prisoners?"

"They are dangerous outlaws! They will both be taken and hanged in a public place!" shouted John.

"The only laws that we respect are the laws of the heart and the laws of King Richard!" protested Robin. "And we are going to die for that?"

"It won't be necessary for you to die, brave Robin," said the black knight calmly. "It is time that order was restored in this country and it looks as if my task will be a hard one."

At these words, he calmly removed his helmet.

"Father, at last you have come home!" cried Marion, weeping for joy.

King Richard's guards arrested Prince John and his men. Then Richard the Lionheart dismounted from his horse and himself untied Lady Marion and Robin Hood. He hugged his daughter and then he said to Robin:

"The fame of your deeds has spread abroad, and I am grateful that you have defended me so bravely. Come with me to my castle. I will make you head of my army."

"Sire, I thank you, but I am not made for the army or for castles," replied Robin. "Sherwood Forest is my domain and for me it is the finest of palaces. However, this palace needs a queen. Your Majesty, I request the hand of your daughter, Marion."

"I am happy to grant it, Robin, and henceforth I will think of you as my son."

Then King Richard turned towards his brother and said severely:

"As for you, John, I order you to leave England at once and never to come back. I will spare your life, but hurry. Go before I change my mind."

That is when England was restored to peace and plenty. Robin Hood and Marion lived together happily and reigned for a long time over the finest of forests.

THE END

The Little Mermaid

ONCE UPON A TIME, AT THE BOTTOM OF THE sea, there was a wonderful kingdom populated by mermaids. The water was so clear that it seemed like crystal. On the rocks many rainbow-coloured shellfish kept opening and shutting with the ebb and flow of the currents, and each one contained a pearl so precious that it would have made the ruler of the richest kingdom turn pale with envy. At the deepest depth stood the King of the Mermaids' castle. The King had six daughters. Each one was beautiful, but the youngest was by far the fairest of all: her skin was as clear and silky as a rose petal and her eyes were as blue as a lagoon. Sadly, her mother had died shortly after the Little Mermaid's birth, but she had been brought up by her grandmother, who loved her dearly and was respected throughout the kingdom.

The Little Mermaid was a strange child, quiet and solitary.
While her sisters played tirelessly among the seaweed with fishes
and dolphins, she spent her time dreaming.

"Alas," she sighed, "why haven't I got legs like human beings,
so that I could run about on the beach and in the countryside?
Instead, all I have is this horrible fish-tail and I must live
under water."

Actually, the Little Mermaid was very pretty
with her silver scales, which shone when a
sunbeam filtered down through the water.

104

One day her grandmother told her:

"When you are fifteen, you will be allowed to go up to the surface of the sea. You can sit there by moonlight on a rock and watch the great ships passing."

These words made the Little Mermaid daydream even more. Alas, she was the youngest.

"I'm only ten. I'll have to wait five long years before I discover the earth!"

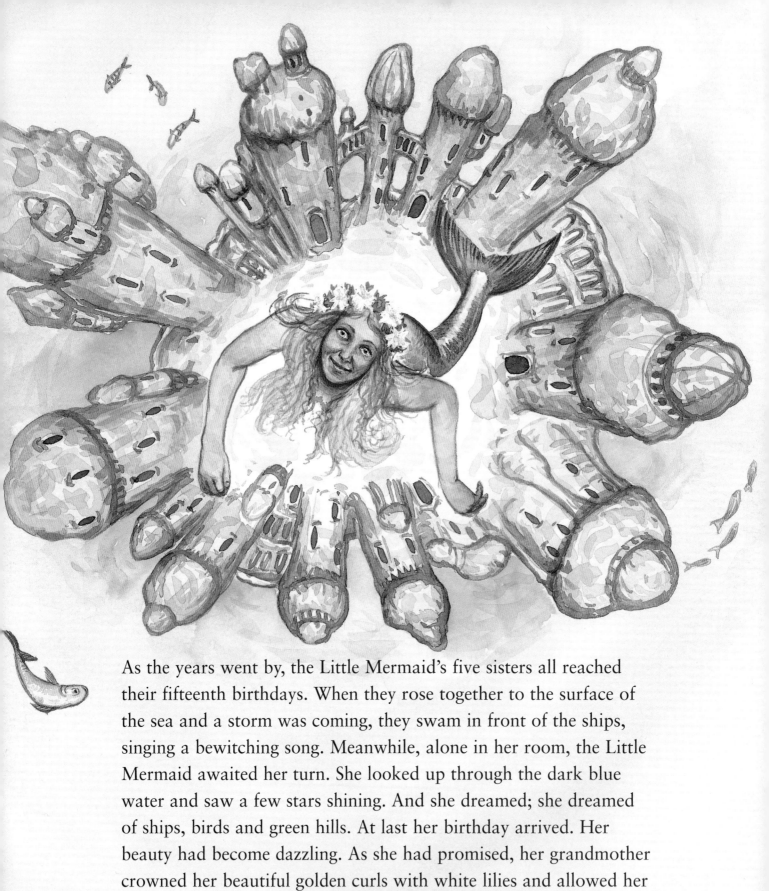

As the years went by, the Little Mermaid's five sisters all reached their fifteenth birthdays. When they rose together to the surface of the sea and a storm was coming, they swam in front of the ships, singing a bewitching song. Meanwhile, alone in her room, the Little Mermaid awaited her turn. She looked up through the dark blue water and saw a few stars shining. And she dreamed; she dreamed of ships, birds and green hills. At last her birthday arrived. Her beauty had become dazzling. As she had promised, her grandmother crowned her beautiful golden curls with white lilies and allowed her to swim up to the surface. Without losing a moment, the Little Mermaid said goodbye to the sea kingdom and thrust upwards, higher and higher towards the sky.

Her heart swelled with joy because at last her dream was coming true. The sun had just set when she reached the surface. The clouds were still glowing pinky-gold and the evening star was shining down on her. Suddenly she saw a big ship not far off. On the bridge the sailors were singing and dancing. The Little Mermaid, who was very curious, swam up to the ship's portholes and pulled herself up to look through the glass. Inside, some men were talking, laughing and singing round a sumptuous feast. Among them was one very handsome young man.

He was a young prince and they were celebrating his birthday.
The prince was so handsome that the Little Mermaid felt her heart
pounding. She had fallen in love. She stayed for a long time looking
through the porthole, wide-eyed with admiration.

Then suddenly she heard a great rumble. The wind rose and the ship
began to rock wildly. A terrible storm was brewing. The sea turned
black. The panic-stricken sailors ran onto the bridge shouting:

"Furl the sails! Bear to port! Bear to starboard!"

A terrifying lightning flash ripped through the sky, followed by an
enormous clap of thunder.

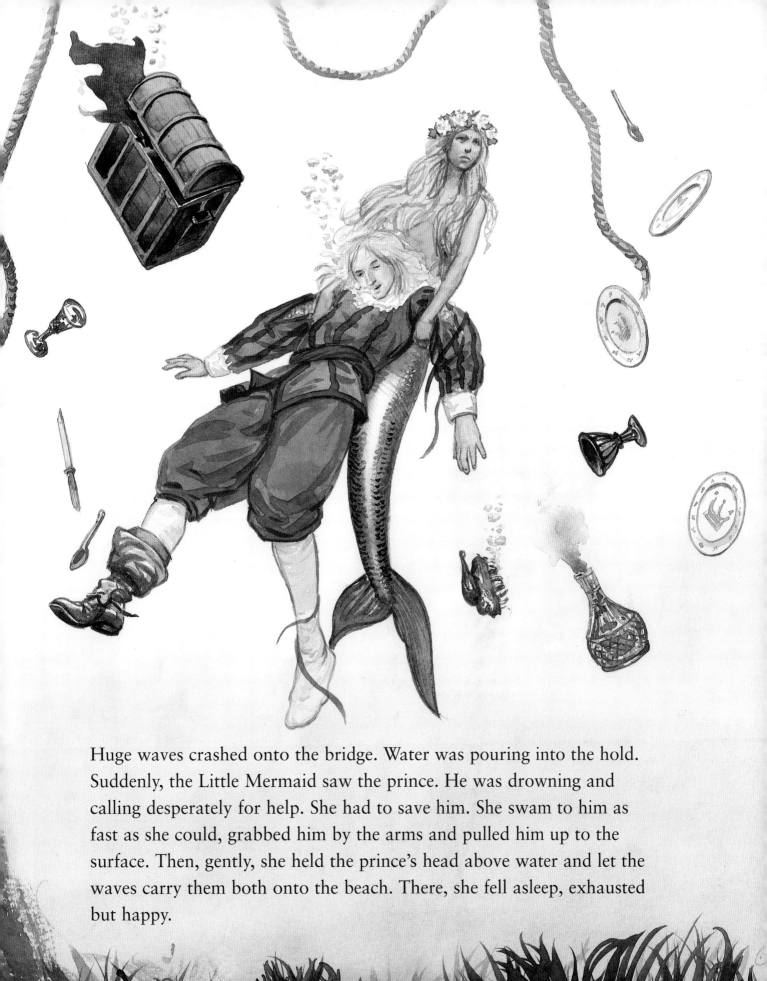

Huge waves crashed onto the bridge. Water was pouring into the hold. Suddenly, the Little Mermaid saw the prince. He was drowning and calling desperately for help. She had to save him. She swam to him as fast as she could, grabbed him by the arms and pulled him up to the surface. Then, gently, she held the prince's head above water and let the waves carry them both onto the beach. There, she fell asleep, exhausted but happy.

Next morning at sunrise, the Little Mermaid awoke. The prince lay beside her, on the sand, sleeping peacefully. She found him so handsome that she couldn't stop herself from placing a tender kiss on his noble forehead. But day was breaking, and the Little Mermaid had to return to her kingdom under the sea. Before she dived, she turned back one last time to look at the prince she loved. It was then that she saw a girl approaching him. The girl leaned over the prince and softly woke him up.

"He will never know that it was I who saved him," the Little Mermaid thought sadly. "He will never recognize me."

She let fall a tear and disappeared into the sea. But each night after that, the Little Mermaid went back to the place where she had left the prince, and each night she sang of her love for him.

Her voice was so beautiful that all the sea creatures came to listen to her. But alas, the prince never heard her. His castle was too far away and the Little Mermaid could go no further than the sandy shore. One day she told her grandmother:

"I am prepared to give up my mermaid's life to make the prince love me. Tonight I will go and find the Sea Witch and ask her to give me legs instead of my fish-tail. Then I will be able to walk till I find the prince's castle and tell him that it was I who saved him. And I'll tell him that I love him."

Her grandmother tried in vain to dissuade
her, as the Little Mermaid had already made up her
mind, and next day she set off for the magic cave where the Sea
Witch lived. It was a dark hole at the very bottom of the sea, where
the sun's rays never reached, the silence was deathly, the water was
murky and the fish were a sad, grey colour. When the Little
Mermaid arrived at the cave, the Sea Witch said to her:

"I know why you have come. Are you ready to give up your
sweet mermaid life just for two ridiculous legs?"

The Little Mermaid
turned very pale as she replied:

"Yes, I am. I'm in love with a prince and I want to go and find him in his castle. To do that I need legs, like humans have."

At this the Sea Witch heated an enormous cauldron.

"Here is your potion, Little Mermaid," said the witch, and handed her a flask of liquid from it. "Drink it tomorrow morning at sunrise: your fish-tail will divide itself and become two legs. Then you will be able to go and find your prince. But remember this: if you do not succeed in making him love you, on the day that he marries someone else, you will be turned into sea foam."

The Little Mermaid
could not imagine such a
tragic outcome. How could
the prince she loved, and had saved, marry any other but herself? So
she picked up the magic potion and prepared to leave, but suddenly
the Sea Witch stopped her:

"Wait a moment, pretty one. If you want this potion, first you'll have
to pay me. You have the most beautiful voice in the sea and you must
surrender it to me."

The Little Mermaid hesitated a moment, but she loved the prince too
much to refuse. So she opened her pretty mouth. Using a sharp blade, the
witch cut out her tongue and the Little Mermaid could speak or sing
no more. She swam up to the beach and waited for the dawn.

As soon as the sun's first rays appeared, the Little Mermaid opened the flask, and swallowed its contents in one gulp. Immediately, she felt as if a sword had pierced her body. She fainted with pain and fell down on the sand. As the sun rose higher and its warm rays beamed down on her, the Little Mermaid awoke to find her tail had gone and she had turned into a real girl.

Gradually, she realized a soft sweet voice was speaking to her. The prince was there, leaning over her. "Who are you?" he asked.

The Little Mermaid wanted to answer, to tell him that it was she who had saved him from drowning and that she loved him. But then she remembered she had lost her tongue.

The prince took the Little Mermaid's hand and led her home to his castle. He dressed her in magnificent robes and presented her at Court. He called her "my little foundling" and treated her very tenderly, but the idea of marrying her did not enter his head.

"I am fond of you," he told her one day, "because you look like the girl who saved my life after a terrible storm. She found me dying on the beach and soon I am going to marry her, because she is my one true love."

These words cut the Little Mermaid to the heart. She tried to make the prince understand that it was she who had saved him, but despite all her efforts, she was unable to utter a word. In despair, the Little Mermaid ran away back to the beach. Days went by. At the castle, preparations were being made for the prince's wedding to the girl who had found him collapsed upon the sand. Sitting alone on a rock by the sea, the Little Mermaid wept bitterly for the man she loved. She knew she could never make him understand and that she had abandoned her family and lost her wonderful voice all for nothing.

The evening of the prince's wedding arrived. From her rock, the Little Mermaid saw the castle's twinkling lights. The celebrations ended very late into the night, when the young bride and groom went to bed. Then the Little Mermaid felt a terrible pain. Her body became light as a feather and broke into a thousand little silver stars. She saw a host of transparent creatures floating in the air beside her and realized that she had turned into foam as the Sea Witch had foretold.

"We are the daughters of the air," her transparent companions told her. "Because you have shared the goodness in your heart we welcome you to come with us to the spirit world."

Now that she was invisible, the Little Mermaid flew to the castle and dropped one last kiss on the forehead of the prince she loved. The wind rose and the Little Mermaid was carried off into the sky forever.

THE END

William Tell

ONCE UPON A TIME, IN A MOUNTAINOUS
country that we call Switzerland today, there was a village
called Altdorf. At that time Switzerland was ruled by her
powerful neighbour, Austria. To establish his authority, the Emperor
of Austria had sent bailiffs into each part of Switzerland, charged
with overseeing the population. These bailiffs were merciless, forcing
the villagers to work by strict rules, stealing their cattle and burning
their cottages. The cruellest of them all was called Gessler, and he
ruled over Altdorf.

In this village full of flowers, beside a great lake, lived a man called William Tell. He was so tall and strong that when he walked out with his little six-year-old son beside him, he looked like a giant. William Tell was very brave and skilful, being the best sailor on the lake and the best bowman in the region. He hunted deer to the tops of the highest mountains. His adventures were talked about in all the market places and everyone in the country loved and respected him.

However, there was one person who hated him and looked on him as his personal enemy: this was the cruel bailiff Gessler. He was afraid of William Tell's strength and courage and his secret wish was to be able to throw William Tell into prison.

120

William was well aware that Gessler's hatred for him was growing day by day. Anxious for his family, he decided to go off and live on the mountain in a wooden hut. There, William spent his days peacefully hunting, while his son, Walter, watched over their flock of goats.

Then, one day, William Tell went down to Altdorf and came across a curious sight. In the middle of the church square there stood a pole so high that no one could ignore it. At the top of this pole there was a hat bearing the Austrian crown. Every villager who passed by the pole stopped and bowed low to the hat, as if it had been the Emperor or the bailiff Gessler in person. And people bowed so respectfully that William Tell, who had been watching this nonsense for a while, burst out laughing.

"Tell me," he asked a merchant, "what has become of our good villagers? Have they gone mad, bowing down before that wooden pole with a common hat on top, or is it some kind of game?"

"Hush! Not so loud, William, because, alas, it is not a game but a new idea of the bailiff's to humiliate us. One of his soldiers came yesterday and read a proclamation: 'Everyone who passes by the hat must bow down before it on pain of death. Signed Gessler, Imperial Bailiff of Austria.'"

At these words, William Tell
abruptly stopped laughing. He took his little boy
by the hand and strode across the square, shouting loud and
clear for all to hear:

"Me, William Tell, bow to a hat? Never! And especially
not Gessler's!" But no sooner had he said these words than a
troop of soldiers burst out from behind the church. They
surrounded William Tell, aiming their bows at him. Then they
marched him off to Gessler, who was surveying the market place
on horseback.

"My Lord, here is a man we have arrested," said one of the
soldiers. "He refused to bow down to the hat."

123

"Well, if it isn't William Tell," said Gessler. "So, we meet again. But explain yourself, why won't you obey your bailiff?"

"I am a free man, living in free country, sir," William replied calmly, holding his head up high.

"What do you mean 'free', William Tell? Can't you see these soldiers? So where's your freedom? I can throw you into prison whenever I like or even condemn you to death."

"But death is also freedom, sir!" said William, defiantly.

"You may be brave, William Tell, but it won't do you any good. I feel like amusing myself a little at your expense. I will spare your life on one condition … I am told that you are the best bowman in the whole of Switzerland."

At these words, the child's face lit up:

"It's true, my Lord! My father is the best," he cried. "Do you see that apple tree over there? Well, my father can split an apple from a hundred paces away. I've never seen him fail, I promise you."

"What's your name, boy?" asked the bailiff, looking down on him with a grim smile.

"Walter Tell," replied the child, proudly.

"Well, Walter, I've got an idea that will amuse me, and you, too. I like to see children enjoying themselves," said the bailiff cruelly. "Go and pick an apple from that tree, then stand with your back to the tree, facing us. Balance the apple on top of your head, and from where he is standing here, your father must split the apple with his arrow."

"I refuse!" exclaimed William Tell.

"William Tell, you will split the apple on your son's head because I order you to do so. Otherwise both of you will die."

An agonized voice then cried out from among the crowd:

"No! Have pity, my Lord, don't do that!"

"Who is that who dares to say no to me?" roared
the bailiff.

"My Lord, I am Edwige, William Tell's wife and Walter's
mother. You cannot order a father to risk murdering his son!
Have pity, sir! Have you no children?" asked the poor woman,
kneeling down before the bailiff.

"Take this mad woman away!" Gessler shouted to his solders.

It was then that young Walter spoke up firmly in his
small voice:

"Mother, don't kneel down to this man.
I shall place the apple on my head,
because I know that Father will succeed.
I trust him."

And the little boy
was as good as his word.
He stood quite still against the tree,
and looked proudly straight ahead.
Ashen-faced, William Tell glanced
at the bailiff and his eyes filled
with tears. But he recovered
himself, and slowly took an arrow from his
quiver. He drew up his bow and aimed
carefully at the apple. The crowd held its
breath. The silence was so intense that
you could hear the arrow whistling
through the air towards Walter. Then
suddenly, the apple cracked, split in two and fell at
the child's feet.

"Bravo! Hurrah! The arrow
has split the apple and the child is
alive! Long live William Tell! Long live
William Tell!" roared the crowd.

Despite the protests
of the crowd, William
Tell was put in chains.
His crossbow, quiver and arrows were
taken away from him and handed to a soldier. The prison loomed darkly on the
other side of the lake. For extra security, the bailiff decided to accompany William
Tell there himself, and they all boarded the boat for the far shore.

They had reached the middle of the lake when suddenly a storm brewed up.
The lake waters grew wild, the wind raised waves as high as mountains and the
boat ran dangerously close to the shore, threatening at any moment to
crash onto the rocks. The soldiers, who were poor sailors, were
panic-stricken.

"Only one man can save us!" cried one soldier. "Our prisoner, William Tell, is the best sailor in the country. We must set him free."

"Yes! Let's free William Tell!"

The bailiff agreed. They unchained William and calmly and confidently, he took charge and began giving orders to the crew, telling them how to steer the craft. Within a few minutes the boat had arrived safely in a bay, out of reach of the storm. William Tell guided it towards a big rock. As soon as it came near enough, he grabbed his bow from the soldier who was looking after it, jumped overboard and gave the boat an almighty push, so that it sailed out of the bay again and back into the storm. William himself escaped inland.

With great difficulty, Gessler and his crew finally came ashore. Meanwhile, William Tell headed over mountains and through forests until he came to a high point overlooking a road. There he waited in hiding, for he knew perfectly well that the bailiff had to pass that way to get back to his castle. As Gessler came along the road, William Tell jumped out of his hiding place. Then he looked the bailiff straight in the eye, loaded his bow, and let fly the arrow. Shot through the heart, the bailiff collapsed and died.

Quick as lightning and agile as a deer, William Tell managed to escape before the soldiers could give the alarm. For a few weeks he remained hiding in the forest, waiting for the hunt to die down. Then finally, calm returned to the region and William returned to the mountain where his wife and son were living. A few years later, Switzerland freed itself from Austrian rule. The bailiffs went back to their own country and the inhabitants of Altdorf were able once again to live in peace, freedom and happiness. Thanks to his courage and his pride, William Tell had become a hero throughout the whole country.

THE END

Cinderella

ONCE UPON A TIME, IN A GREAT KINGDOM, a gentleman lived happily with his wife, who was sweet and good, and his pretty little daughter. But alas, one day, the gentleman's wife fell ill and died. A few years passed, and the gentleman married again, a lady who was cruel, wicked and proud. She had two daughters who were as cruel, wicked and proud as herself. As soon as she saw her, this wicked woman hated her husband's daughter, because the girl's goodness and kindness showed up the stupidity, pride and laziness of her own two. The day after her wedding, the stepmother ordered the poor child to do all the hard work of the household.

She had to scour the pots, wash the dishes and clean the floors. And she scrubbed and polished her stepmother's and her two stepsisters' rooms.

She slept at the top of the house in a
dusty old attic. To reach it she had to climb
up a narrow, ill-lit staircase. When she had finished her work, the
poor child used to sit in the chimney corner, among the cinders, where it was
warm. That was why they called her Cinderella. She enraged her stepsisters
even more, because even in rags with her untidy hair, she was a thousand
times more beautiful than these vain creatures, who spent their days looking
in the mirror and arranging their hair. Cinderella was very unhappy, but she
was so brave that she never complained.

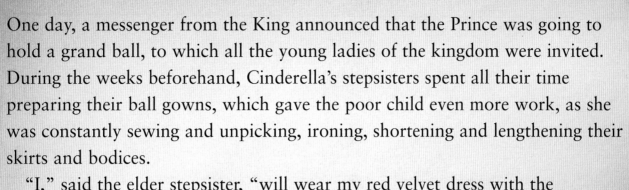

One day, a messenger from the King announced that the Prince was going to hold a grand ball, to which all the young ladies of the kingdom were invited. During the weeks beforehand, Cinderella's stepsisters spent all their time preparing their ball gowns, which gave the poor child even more work, as she was constantly sewing and unpicking, ironing, shortening and lengthening their skirts and bodices.

"I," said the elder stepsister, "will wear my red velvet dress with the silver collar."

"I," said the other, "will wear my gold-embroidered cloak and my diamond tiara."

The two sisters forced Cinderella to be present whenever they tried on their clothes, as they knew she had very good taste.

"Would you like to go to the ball, Cinderella?" asked the younger stepsister.

"Oh! I beg you, don't make fun of me. Look at my hair and my ragged clothes."

"Cinderella is right," said the elder sister. "She would look ridiculous and put us to shame."

Almost anybody would have tried to get her own back for such an insult, but Cinderella, who was not vengeful, took even more trouble to prepare their clothes. At last the evening itself arrived and the two sisters left for the ball, dressed in lavishly embroidered gowns glittering with jewels. From the window of her miserable attic, Cinderella watched them go for as long as she could and then, when the carriage was out of sight, she burst into tears.

From her far-off country, Cinderella's fairy godmother heard her goddaughter crying. With a wave of her magic wand she arrived in the dusty attic.

"What is the matter, my gentle goddaughter?" she asked.

"Oh! Godmother, I would so love to go to the ball," Cinderella replied, in tears.

"Well, you shall go to the ball, and you will be the most beautiful woman there. Go into the garden and fetch a pumpkin."

Although she was very surprised to be asked to do this, Cinderella went out and cut a big pumpkin.

With a wave of her magic wand, the fairy turned it into a magnificent golden coach.

"Now, my pretty child, I need a rat and some mice."

Cinderella brought a big rat and six little mice
from the mousetrap. With another wave of
her magic wand, the fairy turned the mice
into six fine dapple-grey horses, and the big
rat into an elegant coachman.

"Go back out into the garden once more.
Behind the watering can you will find six
brightly coloured lizards. Bring them to me," said
the fairy.

And when Cinderella came back, her fairy godmother turned the
reptiles into smart footmen.

"Now you are ready to go to the ball," said the fairy, admiring the
carriage proudly.

"I don't want to abuse your kindness, dear godmother, but dressed as I am I look like a beggar."

"Oh, dear! What am I thinking of?" cried the good fairy, and she waved her wand again and again until she had turned Cinderella into the most ravishing princess. Her old shirt, full of holes, became a sparkling gold silk robe. Her hair was elegantly styled with curls and intertwined plaits. Then the fairy gave Cinderella a pair of glass slippers that fitted the shape of her pretty little feet perfectly. But her fairy godmother had a word of warning for her:

"Take care, Cinderella! There is one thing you must not forget. Before the twelfth stroke of midnight you must have come home from the ball, otherwise your coach will turn back into a pumpkin, your horses back into mice, your coachman back into a rat, your footmen back into lizards and your magnificent clothes back into rags."

With a grateful heart, the lovely Cinderella promised that she would
obey her godmother and be home by the time the clock struck
midnight. Then she stepped gracefully into her carriage, which rolled
off into the night towards the palace and the Prince's ball.

When Cinderella entered the ballroom, there was a sudden silence:
the violins stopped playing, conversations ceased, and dumb-struck
with admiration, everyone gazed at the dazzling beauty of this unknown
lady. The Prince himself begged her to sit in the place of honour, but then
he found himself unable to utter a single word because he was so enchanted
by her. However, eventually he invited her to dance and Cinderella did so
with such grace that everyone admired her even more. Then, very politely,
she went to greet her sisters, who did not recognize her.

Time seemed to fly by until
Cinderella heard the palace clock striking eleven.

Immediately, she made a graceful curtsey and left the ballroom as fast as she could. As soon as she reached home, she called upon her fairy godmother.

"How can I thank you, dear Godmother? I have just had the happiest time of my life. But I have one more thing to ask you: the Prince invited me to a second ball, which is to be held tomorrow night."

The good fairy was about to answer, when Cinderella's two stepsisters knocked at the front door. Cinderella went to open it for them, rubbing her eyes, as if she had just woken up.

143

"How late you are,
sisters!" she said,
stretching and yawning.
"We had a wonderful
time," said the younger
stepsister. "An unknown princess
came, who was very pleasant to us. She obviously
noticed at once that we are the sort of people to be seen with."

"Nobody knows her name," continued the elder. "We heard that the
Prince would give everything he possesses to know who she is."

Cinderella smiled and said:

"Please sister, lend me your old yellow dress, so that tomorrow I can
go to the ball to see this beautiful princess."

"What? You go to the ball? Are you mad?" cried one.

"You'd look completely ridiculous! You would make us ashamed,"
said the other.

And sniggering together, the nasty pair went off to bed.

The next evening, Cinderella's fairy godmother waved her magic wand and produced more miracles: she turned a pumpkin into a carriage, mice into horses, a rat into a coachman, lizards into footmen. And she spent even more time than the previous evening in producing Cinderella's gown.

"Tonight you must be even more beautiful than last night," said the fairy. "Instead of curls and plaits you will wear your hair loose. Your dress will be made entirely of lace. As for your shoes, you can wear the same pretty glass slippers as before."

And so Cinderella left for the ball dressed like a queen.

On the palace steps, the Prince stood
waiting impatiently. When he saw Cinderella
arriving, he thought he must be dreaming: she was even more beautiful
than he remembered. Gently, he took her hand in his and they began
dancing, twirling and spinning, gazing constantly into each other's eyes.
Cinderella enjoyed herself so much that she did not hear the clock strike
eleven or even half past eleven. But on the last stroke of midnight, she
tore herself out of the Prince's arms in panic and ran away like a
startled deer.

She ran as fast as she could, dashing at full speed down the great palace staircase. In her haste she lost one of her glass slippers, before she disappeared into the night. As he tried to catch up with her, the Prince found the slipper on one of the stairs. Gently he picked it up, touched it to his lips and then ordered his guards to set out in search of the beautiful unknown princess. But she had vanished completely. Cinderella arrived home out of breath, with no coach, no coachman, no horses and no footmen, and wearing her old worn clothes. All she had left of the magnificent evening was one small glass slipper.

When her stepsisters came home from the ball, Cinderella pretended to have just woken up and asked them if they had seen the beautiful princess again.

"She did come," said the elder sister, "but she ran away without even saying goodbye when the clock struck midnight."

"She ran off so fast," continued the younger, "that she lost one of her glass slippers. The Prince picked it up and he refused to dance or even speak for the rest of the evening. He just sat gazing at the little slipper in his hands."

"He is madly in love with her," continued the eldest, "and in my opinion he will do everything he can to find her again."

Indeed, the very next morning a messenger from the King declared that the Prince would marry the girl whose foot fitted perfectly into the glass slipper. First they tried the shoe on princesses, then duchesses, then all the ladies in the kingdom, but none of them had a delicate enough foot. At last the slipper was brought to the two stepsisters, who also tried in vain to squeeze their feet into it.

"Now it is your turn," said the King's messenger, turning towards Cinderella.

"You are joking," cried the two sisters, laughing unkindly. "Cinderella is just a kitchen maid!"

"I have my orders to try the shoe on all the women in the kingdom," replied the messenger.

He knelt in front of Cinderella and offered the slipper to her. The girl slipped her foot into it and of course, the shoe fitted perfectly. Then Cinderella took the other glass slipper out of her apron pocket and showed it to her stepsisters, who were astounded.

Then the fairy godmother arrived, and with a wave of her magic wand, she turned Cinderella's rags into a dress that was even more beautiful than the previous ones. The two cruel sisters recognized the beautiful princess they had seen at the ball and they fell on their knees and begged her forgiveness. Cinderella hugged them and said she forgave them with all her heart. Then Cinderella was taken to the palace where the Prince immediately recognized his fair unknown princess. He found her more beautiful than ever, clasped her in his arms and swore to love her forever. He married her and they had many children.

Cinderella, who was as good as she was beautiful, brought her stepsisters to live at the palace too and, within a year, she married them to two of the lords at court.

THE END

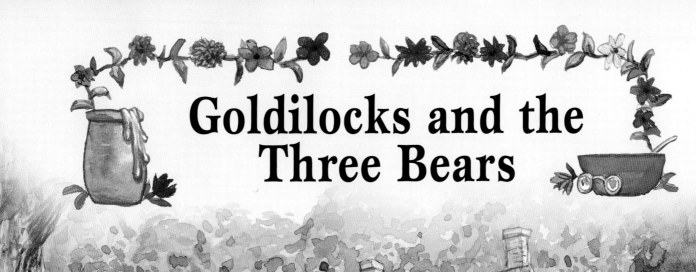

Goldilocks and the Three Bears

ONCE UPON A TIME, THERE WAS A LITTLE GIRL who lived in a pretty little house in a clearing in a forest. Because of her beautiful golden, curly hair, she was called Goldilocks. "Goldilocks," her mother told her, "never go alone into the forest. You never know what might happen." As the little girl was very obedient, she did not go beyond the forest clearing around her house.

But one day, as she was walking in the
grassy clearing, she saw a pretty blue flower growing under the trees.
She took three steps and picked it. A little further into the forest, she saw
a white flower, even more beautiful than the blue one. She took three more
steps and picked that too. Still further on, she discovered a great carpet of
blue and white flowers and ran to pick handfuls of them. When she had
gathered a big enough bunch, she decided to go home and give them to
her mother. But which was the right way home? She chose a path at
random and quickly became lost in the great forest.

Poor Goldilocks walked a long, long way. The birds twittered round her, the wind played in the branches, and waterfalls sang as they bounced over the big pebbles. But the little girl was anxious and very tired. She was just about to burst into tears, when suddenly, through the trees, she saw a little house in the middle of a clearing.

Goldilocks tiptoed up to it. She peered through the window and saw that the house was very clean and tidy. She wondered who lived there. As she could not see anyone, she turned the little door handle and went inside.

The room smelled of cooking and Goldilocks
realized that she was very hungry after her
long walk through the forest.

She went up to the table. It was laid
with a white tablecloth, on which three
bowls of porridge stood side by side:
one big, one medium and one
small. First, she tasted the
porridge in the big bowl, but
it was much too hot.

Then she tasted the porridge
in the medium bowl, but
that was too salty.

Finally, she tasted the porridge in the small
bowl. It was neither too hot nor too salty
but just right. Goldilocks was so hungry
that she ate up the whole bowl, right
down to the last spoonful.

Around the table, there were three chairs, a big one, a medium one and a small one. Goldilocks stood on tiptoe and heaved herself up onto the big chair, but she found it too hard.

Then she tried the medium chair, but she found that one too soft. Finally, she tried the small chair, which she found neither too hard nor too soft, but just right. She leaned back in it.

Crack! The small chair broke under her weight and Goldilocks fell on the floor. Leaving the chair in pieces on the floor, she decided to continue exploring the house.

Goldilocks went upstairs into the bedroom, where she found three beds: a big one, a medium one and a small one. As she was very tired, she lay down on the big bed, but it was much too wide and long for her.

Then she tried the medium bed, but feathers were coming out of the eiderdown and she kept sneezing.

Then she lay on the small bed. It was just the right size for her and lovely and cosy. Goldilocks made herself comfortable and fell asleep almost at once.

Meanwhile, the family that lived in the house had been for a walk in the forest, waiting for their porridge to cool. It was a family of bears. The big bear walked in front; he was Daddy Bear. Behind him came the medium bear, Mummy Bear. And they were both followed by their little Baby Bear. They were listening to the birds twittering, the wind playing in the branches and the waterfalls that sang over the pebbles. When they had walked for a good while, they felt quite hungry and decided it was time to go home for their food. They set out on the path that led to their house.

"Hurry!" said Daddy Bear in his big loud voice, striding along. "I'm very hungry."

"I'm starving" said Mummy Bear in her medium voice.

"Wait for me! Wait for me!" called Baby Bear in his small voice, trying to keep up with them on his short little legs.

They went through the door in single file and up to the table. Suddenly, Daddy Bear noticed that his spoon had already been dipped in his great big bowl.

"Someone has been eating my porridge!" he said in his big, loud voice.

Mummy Bear saw that her spoon had also been left in her medium bowl.

"Someone has been stirring my porridge!" she said in her medium voice.

Then little Baby Bear went up to the table, grabbed the corner of the tablecloth and looked into his small bowl.

"Oh no! Someone has been eating my porridge," he said in his small voice, "and has eaten it all up!"

The three bears were certain that an intruder must have been in their house, and they had a good look round. No one had touched the food in the basket, or the plates on the shelf, or the saucepans near the sink. The honey pot was still on the side-board. Little Baby Bear, who now had no porridge, was about to make himself a good thick slice of bread and honey, when Daddy Bear happened to look at his big chair. He saw that the cushion, which was very hard, was out of place.

"Someone has been sitting on my chair!" he said in his big loud voice.

Little Baby Bear was so frightened that he jumped. Luckily, he did not drop the honey pot. He stood on tiptoe and put it back on the dresser.

Next, Mummy Bear looked at her medium chair.

"Someone has been sitting on my chair, too!" she said in her medium voice.

Then Little Baby Bear ran to his small chair and found it flat on the floor.

"Someone has been sitting on my chair," he said in his small voice, "and broken it into bits!"

Angry now, the three bears began searching the whole house for their intruder.
They opened the cupboards. Nobody.

They went down on all fours to look under the table. Nobody.

They hoisted each other up to look on top of the cupboard.
Nobody.

They lit a candle, opened the cellar door and crept downstairs.
Nobody.

They even searched under
the carpet, up the chimney
and behind the doors.

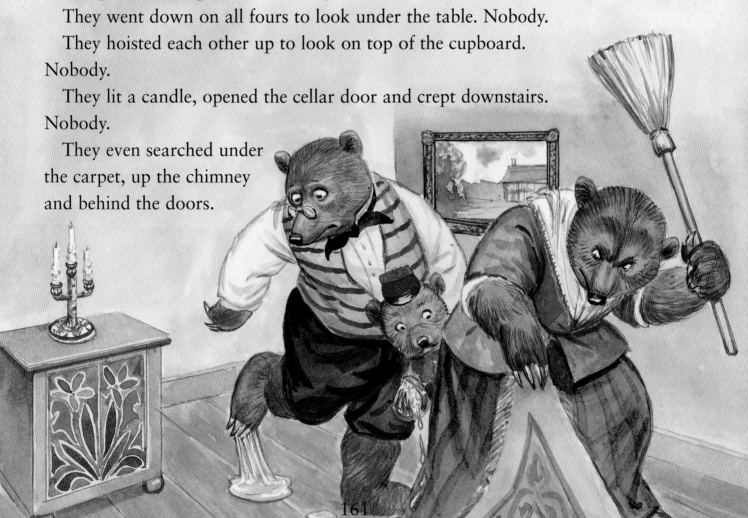

Nobody here. Nobody there. Nobody anywhere. Who then had eaten the porridge? Who had broken the chair?

Daddy Bear, Mummy Bear and little Baby Bear decided to carry on searching. They went upstairs into their bedroom. Daddy Bear went up to his big bed and saw that his pillow was crooked.

"Someone has been lying in my bed!" he said in his big loud voice.

Mummy Bear went up to the medium bed and saw that its sheets were all creased.

"Someone has been lying in my bed, too!" she said in her medium voice.

Little Baby Bear hopped to his little bed. The pillow was straight and the sheets firmly tucked in. But right there, large as life, lay Goldilocks, fast asleep.

"Someone has been lying in my bed and she is still here! Oh!" cried Baby Bear as loud as he could in his small voice.

When she head Daddy Bear's big voice and Mummy Bear's medium voice, Goldilocks thought she was dreaming. But Baby Bear's loud squeak woke her up properly. She sat up in bed and was amazed to see the three bears standing in front of her. Then she screamed, scrambled out of bed and rushed to the open window. She jumped down to the ground and began running for all she was worth.

The three bears were not bad. They did not try to catch or punish her for having eaten Baby Bear's porridge, broken his chair and slept in his bed.

They leaned out of the
window and watched her as she ran off
through the clearing. Daddy Bear called to her in his big loud voice:
"That's what happens when you don't listen to your mother!"
Mummy Bear added in her medium voice:
"You have forgotten your pretty bunch of flowers!"
And Baby Bear leaning out as far as he could, called out in his small voice:
"Hey! Hey, little girl! Take the path
to the right to get out of the wood."

Goldilocks took the path
to the right. She ran through the wood.
She did not stop to hear the birds twittering
or to drink water from the stream. She did not
pick a single flower. She soon arrived safely at the
other end of the forest where she saw her mother
waiting for her in front of her house. She ran and
threw herself into her mother's arms and told her
the story of the blue and white flowers, the
empty house, the porridge that was neither too
hot nor too salty, the broken chair, the cosy
little bed and the three bears.

"So, you see, darling," said her mother,
"if you had listened to me, you would
not have got lost and you would
not have had such a fright."

165

Since then, Goldilocks has learned her lesson. If she is left alone, she never strays far from the house. But each time she looks at the great trees of the forest, each time she picks a flower, she remembers her strange adventure.

"Baby Bear was very kind," she thinks. "But for him, I would never have found my way home. And I had eaten all his porridge!"

THE END

Jack and the Beanstalk

ONCE UPON A TIME, IN A FAR AWAY COUNTRY, there lived a boy called Jack. He lived with his mother in a tumbledown thatched cottage surrounded by a little garden. Jack and his mother worked hard, but they were very poor: all they had was a single cow. But the cow was already very old, and one day she stopped giving them any milk. So the poor woman decided to sell the animal.

"Jack, the cow is no use to us any longer and she eats up our hay. Tomorrow you will take her to market. She is not worth much, but all the same, try to get as good a price for her as you can."

Early next morning, Jack tied a rope round the cow's neck and took her to market.

On the way he met an old man dressed in rags, who was limping along bent over a walking stick.

"Where are you going with that cow?" asked the old man.

"I'm going to the village to sell her," replied Jack.

"Well, you don't need to go all the way. If you like, I'll buy your cow from you myself. Look! In exchange I'll give you this bean. But take great care of it, because it's a magic bean! It will bring you wealth and happiness, if you make good use of it," he assured Jack.

Jack thought it over for a moment:

"Well, she's a very old cow and I'm afraid it will be difficult to sell her. I'm not risking much if I accept the old man's proposal. And perhaps I'll find a good way of using that bean!"

So Jack sold his cow for a bean, and hurried home, feeling quite happy with himself. When his mother saw him come in, she said:

"You are looking very pleased with yourself, my son. So, have you brought me lots of money?"

When she saw that all Jack had brought back was one small bean, the good woman flew into a rage.

"But what's going to happen to us? Why is my son so stupid? Go to your room! I don't want to see you again today!" she ordered him.

In her rage, she threw the bean out of the window, then she dropped onto a chair and burst into tears. Jack spent the rest of the day in his room, wishing he hadn't upset his mother so much. When evening came, he fell asleep.

Next morning, Jack got up to open his shutters. But try as
he might with all his strength, he could not push them
open. It was as if they were blocked on the outside. Jack
ran into the garden to see what was in the way and there
… oh, what a surprise! A gigantic beanstalk with huge
leaves had grown up in the night, from the spot
where the bean had fallen. The beanstalk was
higher than the house; it went up higher and
higher till its top was lost in the clouds.

"I am going to climb this beanstalk to see
where it leads to," Jack said to himself.

So, straight away, he began climbing from
branch to branch and leaf to leaf.

He climbed for a long time, higher and higher.
He thought that soon he would touch the sky.
When he reached the top, among the clouds, he
saw a wide path bordered by trees.

Far off stood a magnificent castle.
Jack decided to go there.

When he arrived at the enormous castle door, Jack knocked. A giant of a woman opened the door to him.

"Good morning," he said very politely. "I have come a long way and I am very thirsty and very hungry. Could you give me a big glass of water and something to eat?"

"My poor boy," replied the woman, "you would do better to leave at once, because my husband is a terrible ogre who eats children! If he finds you here, he'll swallow you up in one mouthful!"

Suddenly the castle floor began to shake.

"Quick! He's coming! Hide behind the dresser!" said the woman.

Jack ran and hid. Then he saw an enormous ogre with a cruel face and pointed teeth. In one hand he was carrying a sack and in the other, a sheep. The ogre threw the sack into a corner and some gold pieces fell out. Suddenly, he stopped, his nose twitched and he began sniffing the air in all directions.

"Fee, fie, foe, fum! I smell fresh meat here!" he cried, licking his lips hungrily.

"Of course. It's that sheep you have just brought in.
Give it to me and I'll cook it," replied his wife, trembling
at the thought that her husband might find the boy.
With a suspicious grunt, the ogre sat down in his huge chair and waited
for the meal to be cooked. Then he flung himself greedily upon the sheep
and ate it up, bones and all. Full at last, he went up to bed with his wife
and began snoring so loudly that the whole castle shook.

174

Seizing his opportunity, Jack crept from his hiding place, took the sack full of gold pieces and ran off. The beanstalk was still there, and he slid down it to the ground. Jack's mother had been very worried by his disappearance and rushed out to greet him. He told her about his extraordinary adventure.

"You see, mother, it really was a magic bean. Look! This is for you," he said, giving her the sack full of gold pieces.

Jack's mother thanked heaven for having given her such a clever son. Both of them lived very comfortably for a few months, thanks to the ogre's fortune.

But when all the gold pieces had been spent, Jack decided to go back to the castle at the top of the beanstalk. He climbed from branch to branch and from leaf to leaf to the top of the magic plant. Once again, he knocked at the enormous castle door and begged the ogre's wife to let him in.

"You little rascal! Aren't you ashamed to come back here? Last time you stole a sack full of gold pieces from us! Since then my husband has been in a very bad temper!"

But even before Jack could say a word in reply, the floor began to shake.

"Quick! Hide in the oven!" cried the woman.

Jack leapt through the door and ran to hide in the oven.

"Fee, fie, foe, fum! I smell fresh meat here!" shouted the ogre in a voice of thunder.

"It's that fat pig you have brought in. Give it to me, I'll cook it for you," replied his wife, quickly.

"Yes, I'd love some pork roasted in the oven," said the ogre.

"It will be much better roasted on the spit," his wife advised him.

Fortunately for Jack, the ogre agreed, and his wife roasted the pig on the spit in the fireplace. The hungry ogre swallowed the pig in one mouthful, bones and all.

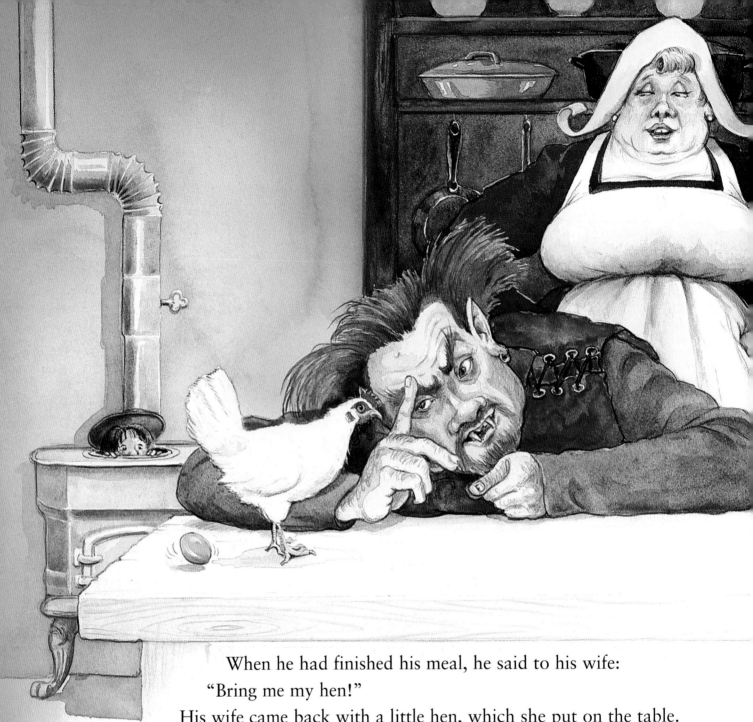

When he had finished his meal, he said to his wife:

"Bring me my hen!"

His wife came back with a little hen, which she put on the table.

"Lay an egg!" the ogre ordered the hen.

And Jack was amazed to see the hen immediately lay a shiny yellow egg: it was a golden egg! The ogre stroked the hen for a moment, then he yawned and went to sit in an armchair, where he fell asleep. Then Jack came out of his hiding place, picked up the hen, put her under his arm, and ran off from the castle as fast as his legs could carry him. Now Jack and his mother no longer had to worry about the future, because the hen laid a golden egg every day. But the months went by, and Jack began to find life very boring, so he decided to go back to the castle once more.

Jack came out of his hiding place, grabbed the harp and made for the door. But, just as he was crossing the threshold, he knocked the harp against the door-frame and its strings jangled. The sound woke the ogre and he gave a shout of rage that made the whole castle quake. He leapt to his feet and rushed off in pursuit of the thief. Jack ran as fast as he could, but the ogre ran after him with great strides and roaring:

"So it was you, you rascal! Beware when I catch you! This time you shan't escape me!"

Jack jumped onto the beanstalk and slid all the way down to the bottom.

Behind him, the ogre clung to the beanstalk as well as he could and tried not to lose sight of the boy. But Jack was much too quick and agile and reached the ground well before him.

"Quick, mother, the ogre is coming! We must cut down the beanstalk," cried Jack.

With an axe and a saw, they both attacked the enormous stem. Suddenly there was a terrible crack and the entire beanstalk collapsed, crushing the giant who was just about to set foot on the ground.

From then on, Jack could never return to the castle. But, thanks to the hen that laid the golden eggs and the sweet music played by the magic harp, he lived for a long, happy time with his mother.

THE END

About the Tales

Fairy tales are folktales, or fables. In them, all kinds of
magical things can happen: beasts become princes, pumpkins
become carriages, and genies appear from lamps. We meet
witches, kings and queens, princes and princesses, giants, talking
animals and sometimes even fairy godmothers.
Although they can sometimes be frightening, fairy tales can
help us to overcome our fears, and often have things to teach us.
Some fairy tales are stories that have been passed down from
parents to children for centuries by word of mouth, and were
not published in books until more recent times when they
were finally written down. Others were created by authors
that we know quite a lot about – you may even
recognize some of the names mentioned in
this part of the book.

BEAUTY AND THE BEAST

Written and spoken versions of the *Beauty and the Beast* story have been around for centuries and, more recently, film and cartoon versions have also been created.

Early tellings of the story were not meant for children. One of these appeared in 1740, written by a woman called Madame Gabrielle de Villeneuve. Madame de Villeneuve wrote fairy tale romances, taken from earlier tales and folklore, to entertain her friends.

When a French aristocrat, Madame Jeanne-Marie Le Prince de Beaumont, came to England in 1745, she began to write books on education and morals for children. She took Madame de Villeneuve's tale and shortened it, creating the version we now know.

Beauty and the Beast helps us to understand that beauty is only skin deep, and that sometimes putting others' needs before our own can be rewarding.

THE PIED PIPER OF HAMELIN

This story – encouraging us to keep our promises, or else! – grew out of a strange, real-life event. To this day, no one is sure what really happened, but an ancient plaque in the German town of Hameln states that on 26 June, 1284, a piper in colourful clothing lead 130 children away from the town, never to be seen again. A street in Hameln, the *Bungelose Gasse* or Drumless Lane, was named after the event, and to this day it is forbidden to sing or play an instrument there out of respect for the children who disappeared all those years ago. Different versions of this folk tale were gathered by the Brothers Grimm in 1812. They were brothers famous for collecting and writing down fairy tales that had been passed down from generation to generation. The story was also famously retold by the poet Robert Browning in 1842 in his poem *The Pied Piper of Hamelin*.

ALADDIN

The story of *Aladdin* and his magic lamp is another of the best-known stories ever written and is part of *The Thousand and One Nights* or *Arabian Nights*. This collection of around 200 folk tales comes from the Indian, Persian and Arab cultures, and dates back to 850 AD.

The version we know appeared for the first time between 1704 and 1717 in a translation by a man called Antoine Galland, a talented French storyteller and professor of Arabic. He translated the tales and changed them to suit the tastes of his French readers, the story of *Aladdin* having been told to him by a Syrian friend and scholar.

Aladdin helps us to realize that we shouldn't take the things we have for granted, and to recognize the true value of what we have.

HANSEL AND GRETEL

The story of *Hansel and Gretel* was first put in writing by the Brothers Grimm in the early nineteenth century. Their version came from a storyteller called Dortchen Wild in the town of Cassel in Germany, who later became Wilhelm Grimm's wife.

There are many different versions of this story to be found around the world, but whoever the main characters are, they are always forced be resourceful, work together and use their courage to overcome their fears.

PETER PAN

The author of *Peter Pan*, James Matthew Barrie, was born in a small weaving town in Scotland in 1860. He was the ninth of ten children of a handloom weaver and his wife. Barrie's older brother, David, died after a skating accident on the eve of his fourteenth birthday. His mother was very upset, but was consoled by the thought that David would always remain a boy. Some people think the idea of this inspired Barrie to write his most famous play, *Peter Pan*. Whether enjoyed as a play, a book or a cartoon, the story of *Peter Pan* encourages us to think about the responsibilities of growing up – or not!

ROBIN HOOD

Famous for robbing from the rich to give to the poor, the story of *Robin Hood* is hugely popular across the world, where his adventures have been translated into many different languages, and made into many films and cartoons.

Born in Lockesley in either Yorkshire or Nottinghamshire in 1160, he first appeared in ballads, or songs, sung in England in the Middle Ages.

England's best-loved outlaw teaches us to help people less fortunate than ourselves, and the value of true friendship.

THE LITTLE MERMAID

This fairy tale about a young mermaid was first published in 1836. It was written by Hans Christian Andersen, who was a Danish author and poet famous for his fairy tales. His father was a shoemaker, and his mother was a washerwoman for rich people with big houses. Hans Christian Andersen grew up to be tall and thin with a big nose, and always considered himself ugly. His stories often show understanding for those who are suffering, or who are different in some way. During his life, Hans Christian Andersen wrote more than 150 fairy tales, which have been translated into over 100 languages, and made into many films and cartoons. A statue of The Little Mermaid sits on a rock in Copenhagen harbour as a symbol of Copenhagen, and of the Danes' pride in their greatest writer.

WILLIAM TELL

William Tell is the tale of a hero who represents the Swiss people's fight for freedom in Medieval times. To this day, no one is sure whether or not he really existed.

Legend has it that he was a peasant from Bürglen, a town in a part of Switzerland called Uri, who fought against the strict Austrian rule of the time. It is believed that William helped the Swiss people to rise up against the Austrians and gain their freedom after being forced to shoot an apple from his son's head by the cruel Austrian bailiff, Gessler, who he eventually kills.

The story of the archer's test is often found in folklore over the centuries. William Tell's exciting adventure encourages us to be brave, have trust in ourselves, and the courage to stand up for what we believe in.

CINDERELLA

Many different cultures around the world have a version of the *Cinderella* story, and the earliest known one comes from China. However, the story we all know today, complete with fairy godmother and pumpkin, dates from the seventeenth century and was written by the French author, Charles Perrault.

One of the most beloved and well-known fairy tales of all time, it has taught generations that true beauty comes from within. The tale also explains how giving, and expecting nothing in return, receives its just reward in the end.

GOLDILOCKS AND THE THREE BEARS

In the earliest version of this tale, an old woman called 'Silver Hair' sneaks into the bears' home to taste their food and try out their beds. Goldilocks didn't become the naughty little girl we all know today until 1849. She became 'Silver-Locks' when she was transformed from an old woman to a young girl, then 'Golden Hair' and, eventually, in 1904, she was christened 'Goldilocks.' The message in the story of *Goldilocks and the Three Bears* is to have respect for other people's property and to listen to your elders!

JACK AND THE BEANSTALK

The young trickster and beanstalk climber, Jack, has been around for some centuries.

Once again, many variations of the tale exist in different countries. The English version, *Jack and the Beanstalk*, is probably the best-known and most popular, and the earliest printed version of the story which has survived is one that appears in a book from 1807 called *The History of Jack and the Bean-Stalk*.

The story of *Jack and the Beanstalk* is really the tale of a boy growing up and learning to make his own choices and decisions.